For Reference

Not to be taken from this room

The Futurist poet, wounded in battle, wonders if he is dying.

In great pain he is first stretchered to a ruined church,

then transported in a lurching automobile.

He describes his experience with a virtuoso use of typeforms.

He seems to have trawled the typebooks of the day to get his effects.

FERITA + OSPEDALE + ETISIA

TRAIETTORI E BOMBARDE
M AGOLIO
NIAA
INDIFFERENZA
sghignazzatatatatata di una mitragliatrice

qo qo qo
DIO oh
MARIA oh
AMMA oh oh oh

ferita al petto
gorgo di parole e di sangue

MUOIO ? CALMA
PACE
SERENITÀ

Perchè non ho orrore del nulla
allora?
Sui capelli la terra smossa da una mitragliatrice che
morde il tronco dell'albero che mi copre

s O le pallido svenuto fra la bambagia
delle nubi

sul mio petto una

r sa
r ssa
come la mia r O ssa ferita come le
labbra r sse della donna che
non ho amato r sso come il mio entu-
siasmo sso come le mostrine
del mitraglie- re terrorizzato
dritto rigido dietro il tronco grosso d'un albero
stagno di sangue in fondo al petto
è amaro **amaro amaro** sputare il proprio sangue
sentire un' calda
Onda salire salire
eccomi in una BaRELLa .calda

CAMPANILE DiROccaTo CHIEsa

S P—EtRo
braaabraaaahhhhh sangue caffè acqua vomitati caldi
giù sul petto nudo
ahrrrrrrr ahrrrrrrr ahrrrr sezione sanità
nera toga cappellano stola **viola** brutte parole
incomprensibili sul corpo dei moribondi dei **MORTI**
tutto **TUTTO UN'URLO**
l'-ah-ahh-ah-ah-menti
ahi! ago lungo grossa siringa antitetanica acqua! acqua!
unica parola urlata
A C Q U A !!
Via! automobile ballonzolio
DOLORE
braaahbrahh sangue sù sù amaro in bocca giù
fra la barba sporca Ho sete ahi! Ho sete

JAMAR 14
Futurista ferito al fronte.

A group of British travellers study remains of the Ancient World in 1751.

They weren't the first to have been inspired by that world. A not always accurate idea of ancient Rome greatly influenced the Italian Renaissance and decided, amongst much else, the form of roman type. Later, an enthusiasm for 'primitive' Greece and Rome fashioned much of eighteenth-century England. The creation of an architecture to reflect this, and a desire to incorporate the correct lettering for that architecture, produced those sanserifs and grotesques which play such an important part in our lives today. These foppish gentlemen in the wilds may not have been correct in their belief that antiquity was an era of the Noble Savage and barbaric forms, but their creative response has had a long-lasting effect.

Alan Bartram   **Typeforms   a history**

The British Library & Oak Knoll Press 2007

First published 2007 by
The British Library
96 Euston Road
London NW1 2DB
and by
Oak Knoll Press
310 Delaware Street
New Castle
DE 19720

Cataloguing-in-publication Data
Catalogue records for this book are available
from The British Library and the Library of
Congress
ISBN 978-0-7123-0971-4 (BL)
ISBN 978-1-58456-222-1 (OKP)

Designed by Alan Bartram
Typeset in Monotype Fournier
and Franklin Gothic Heavy
by Norman Tilley Graphics, Northampton
Printed in England at the University Press,
Cambridge

ACKNOWLEDGEMENTS
My thanks to Phil Baines and John Trevitt for
their comments on the typescript. And to
Lucy Myers of Lund Humphries, publishers
and copyright holders of the original *Atlas of
Typeforms*, for permission to re-use some of
the material. I am indebted to my co-author
of that earlier volume, James Sutton, for much
of his contribution there is incorporated here.
And especial thanks to John Taylor, our
understanding and committed publisher at
Lund Humphries all those years ago.
    The Futurist poem on page 1 is from
L'Italia Futurista, 1916-18.
    The frontispiece is from *The Antiquities of
Athens*, volume 3, 1794. The background to
this can be found in *Building on Ruins: the
rediscovery of Rome and English architecture*
by Frank Salmon, 2000.
    My photographs of architectural and
vernacular lettering are now deposited with
the Central Lettering Record, of which Phil
Baines is curator.

Contents

This book is partly based on *An Atlas of Typeforms* (which James Sutton and I wrote in 1968), abridged and mostly rewritten; to it is added a parallel story of architectural and vernacular lettering. That book came out in a world unlike today's. The intervening forty years have seen major changes brought about by technology; changes in society and the economy which encouraged the dominance of profit over 'worthwhileness'; and changes in commercial preferences that effectively brought an end to my parallel story. Much of this present book is history; but for a full understanding of type today, we need to know that history.

The *Atlas* was published in the very sunset of metal type and letterpress printing. The types shown here are those metal types, for they are often historically more revealing than today's digital designs derived from them. Many of the post-1750 types I show are either from the original punches or matrices, or very close copies of the originals. Thus, when I compare these with the lettering of my parallel story – architectural or vernacular forms – any relationship is a valid one; for the new technology and digitisation created problems which had to be overcome by some modification of the metal form. I discuss this and show some such changes at the end of the book.

That changing technology was initially – it is generally agreed – a disaster. Types were badly adapted for filmsetting – as it was then – and print quality was generally dull and flat. The printed type was grey and insipid, lacking the sparkle and richness of good letterpress, and halftones were drab. It was, on the whole, not a happy episode in printing history. The story today is different. Illustrations are rich in tone and colour; detail is retained, allowing (if need be) illustrations to be quite small without loss of meaning. We now take it for granted that illustrations and their related text are placed together, and forget the time when pictures were bunched up in a distant part of the book, as so often happened, for technical reasons, in the days of letterpress. Type is now

properly black and crisply printed, although unfortunately, as I explain later, some old friends were digitised in a form that often makes them too light, especially in smaller sizes. Recently, some 'second generation' versions have appeared, aiming to be more authentic. Yet it matters not how faithful they are to the originals: they merely need to be usable.

But against any disappointments can be set the control a knowledgeable designer has over the typesetting itself. AppleMacs and their kin allow all Geoffrey Dowding's *Finer Points in the Spacing and Arrangement of Type* of 1954 to be implemented following the designer's personal preferences and idiosyncrasies, of which most good typographers have a sackful, bitterly upheld and contested, with zero tolerance for alternative views.

Previously, the designer was to some extent at the mercy of the compositor, who might have been both ignorant and careless. But more often, in the book trade, he was not. He not only set the type, but made a contribution that today should be done – but is often not done – by a publisher's house editor – an essential member of the production team who frequently seems to have gone missing. That compositor of yesterday would correct punctuation, grammar, spelling, and even query facts, for they were highly trained craftsmen, having served a six-year apprenticeship in a trade that jealously guarded its skills. Many authors today, because they own an AppleMac, believe, in their ignorance, that they can design and set their own books, which they can, of course, but badly.

Today we have to work as if we had undergone the long years of apprenticeship that those men in the printer's composing room had experienced. If a designer restricts himself or herself to a few typestyles, enough accumulated knowledge is gained to enable informed decisions on the optimum letter fit, letterspacing and leading for particular sizes to be made. Who needs more than five or six typestyles? A thorough knowledge of and feeling for a few old favourites is better than casual encounters purely for the sake of originality.

When the *Atlas* was published, the designer had to use whatever type the printer or typesetter (usually, then, the same firm) held. Most reputable book printers would hold a workmanlike range of a dozen or so usable types. Not only was type much more expensive than today, each size had to be bought in – or as many sizes as the printer felt he was likely to need. A trade typesetter might hold the hundred or more, in all available sizes and weights, that advertisers demanded. Today, any designer can personally own far more styles than he is ever likely to use. And, of course, sizes can be varied from the one master to an infinitesimal degree, unlike the restrictions imposed by metal type. Yet no-one worth his or her salt then felt constrained by this: imagination or ingenuity, professionalism or good judgement carried you through. You never feel Tschichold or Schmoller, for instance, wished they could change a type size by 0.1pt, or even 0.3pts. Limitations concentrate the mind.

As I say later, the very method of creating a design rough – the tracing off, the tracing down, the painting in – meant that you gained some knowledge of different typeforms as a matter of course. Mere theory and staring at a computer screen, or even at typesheets, are no substitute for a pencil (that outmoded tool) and paper. Creating a paste-up from galleys supplied by a typesetter meant you worked, with paper, at the same size as the final result. We all know those reduced examples of award-winning designs which look so wonderful, but which, seen in real size, are disappointing. With the computer a designer can produce a dozen minutely different variations of a design in seconds; but this would reduce me, who doesn't use one, to a dithering indecisive wreck.

There is no doubt that today the designer, and the printer, have the equipment to create work as good as, and in many ways better than, could ever be achieved in the 'golden age' of yesteryear, for actually it wasn't always so golden. But other aspects of that past were undoubtedly conducive to the creation of more satisfying work. For the response to the cut-throat situation today shows a depressing assessment of the general public's visual preferences.

Marketing. That is the ogre that stalks publishing today. Marketing, men in suits, the bottom line, the moneymen, the bookshop; with Amazon chewing away at them all. It is a battlefield out there. Life is rough and tough. By 2007, nearly 200,000 new titles a year were being published in the UK alone. Somehow, somewhere, someone hopes all these will be sold.

In 1941, Allen Lane was looking at a potential Penguin (*Living in Cities* by Ralph Tubbs, a vision of how blitzed towns and cities could – and should – be rebuilt). He said: 'Our cost of production will amount to almost exactly twice the amount we will receive from the trade, but so convinced am I of the "worthwhileness" of the venture, that this causes me no qualms.' Or, in 1949: 'Quite frankly I don't think we shall make a profit on this book. This does not cause me the slightest concern … as I feel … it is a new landmark.' (The book was *The Archaeology of Palestine*.)

Reading *Penguin Portraits. Allen Lane and the Penguin Editors* by Steve Hare, I was struck by the enthusiasm of these overworked and underpaid people in publishing. (Actually, all three characteristics still exist.) Just after the war, even during it, was an idealistic age: 'we are building a new world'. That was not a hope, but a belief; and publishers played a crucial role in attempting to make the aspiration a reality. 'We fitted into a time of very high idealism – and a wish to share a kind of explosive creativity which was so evident in all the writers and editors who themselves had so much to express, and who needed us as a forum' (Eunice Frost, a Penguin editor).

The designer Colin Banks described Ralph Tubbs, the architect and author of *Living in Cities*, as speaking to us 'with shining eyes, brimming with optimism for a new world order' and asks: 'isn't that what design meant to us all then?' The mid-1940s was when 'commercial art' became graphic design. The seminal typography course of the 1950s at the Central School of Arts and Crafts in London run by Herbert Spencer and Anthony Froshaug was a major force, teaching the New Typography (new in Britain). While Gill Sans was the type of choice (it was readily available), and grotesques – reflecting the Swiss preference – were also popular, a knowledge and awareness of more traditional faces was always considered part of a typographer's essential kit.

The belief that good design made for a better society motivated many designers here and abroad until disillusion set in during the 1960s, by which time it became clear that society had other priorities, despite all the educational and promotional efforts of the Council of Industrial Design (COID) and later bodies. Today such offspring of the 'nanny state' are slagged off; but I have never had a problem with them, or it, believing personally that such nannying is one of the duties of the state. Without this conviction, how could I write books urging a knowledge of design I believe anyone working in this field, or even the general public, should be required to have? One might say, *especially* the general public.

In 1947 the COID suggested to Penguin (that name again) a series of books called *The Things We See* 'to encourage us to look at the objects of everyday life with fresh and critical eyes. Thus, while increasing our own daily pleasure we also become better able to create surroundings that will give us permanent pleasure.' The subjects included houses, furniture, pottery and glass, public transport, ships and printing – subjects 'in which many of us are unaware of the subtle variations in excellence or even the difference between good and bad'. Even if the very concept of 'Good Design' had not become out-of-date, a phrase from the past, I could not imagine such a project being considered today by any of the conglomerates that have each swallowed up four or five once-independent publishers.

In contrast to those takeovers and groupings, the new technology has allowed the setting up of tiny publishers willing to chance their arm (or their money), sometimes rather incautiously. Such kitchen table adventurers, admirable though they are, can be horribly ignorant of the subtleties of typeforms and typography. It would be nice to think that, once the initial excitement has worn off, they feel a desire to know more about type, that versatile tool with which we work. It is not knowledge that simply happens: it requires some effort to attain. If the lack of it becomes the norm, the beginning of a slippery slope beckons. Conversely, the work of just two men, Tschichold and Schmoller, at Penguin from 1947 onwards, *raised* the standard of design and printing for the whole of British publishing, even of printing generally. That happened within the context of a particularly lucky combination of circumstances, a context this Prologue has tried to depict.

Parallel lines never meet, and my two parallel stories of typeforms and architectural/vernacular lettering do not get seriously entangled until the beginning of the nineteenth century. That entanglement seemed to stop coincidentally about the same time as metal type died out, and the world just described became a memory; although there is no suggestion of a causal link. Nonetheless, no continuation of a similar relationship is detectable today, not least because the tradition of vernacular lettering, and the architectural use of lettering, has unfortunately more or less died out.

Perhaps we are too close in time to detect any pattern in contemporary type design, amongst the welter of new forms, yet alone relate them to any parallel story. From today's perspective we can easily see the earlier interaction of different traditions, and their creative consequences. The caps of early typeforms derived ultimately from Roman inscriptions, the lowercase from Renaissance calligraphy which itself had a convoluted history. Such an inheritance broke down in the beginning of the nineteenth century when it was jolted off course by a combination of industrial requirements, and somewhat naive ideas about the Noble Savage and rugged antiquity, which was how the intellectually fashionable Greek world was regarded. But today there is neither a consistent influence of carved or pen forms, nor the intellectual backing of a historical theory. Those 'outside' influences had a reinvigorating effect on type, and type design was an equally beneficial influence on those other forms of lettering. The lack of this happy interaction is impoverishing to both. Looking at it from our close-up viewpoint, there seems now an individualistic free-for-all, not a steady development, on a broad front, of inherited forms or traditions. Such a situation rather reflects the aggressive and competitive society in which the design and publishing worlds now operate. Yet there is a contradiction here, for that aggression seems to be strangely conservative and afraid of the individualism, or the belief in 'worthwhileness', that characterised the small publishers in their calmer world of the 1940s, 1950s and 1960s.

This is a history book. Many new types (far too many) have been produced in the last thirty years, which can be examined in the plethora of type books now available. But one strand of my dual story has disappeared from the scene. The long and vigorous tradition of vernacular lettering in England had been dealt a blow in the early twentieth century by the reverence for Trajan roman initiated by Edward Johnston and some of his disciples. This form was widely adopted in varying degrees of accuracy or sensitivity by organisations – banks, commercial firms, municipal authorities, the Ministry of Works – who felt it conveyed good taste and dignity. The tradition was further weakened by commercial sign-producing firms who could supply the increasingly brash high streets with cheap products in modern (that is, plastic) form, normally using a debased typeface.

The self-employed journeyman, creating many different styles of his own, travelling the country, shouting at the top of his voice, as one voluble Irish signwriter put it, that he is happy with his existence, is no longer in demand. And the rare architect with an interest in lettering is not usually bold enough (or is not allowed by local planning authorities) to design or commission innovative forms.

The English lettering tradition crossed the Atlantic seemingly as early as the mid-eighteenth century, if not earlier. As Paul Shaw has suggested, in the journal *Forum*, emigrating lettercarvers could have been partly responsible. There are tombstones dated between 1750 and 1800 in Manhattan that suspiciously resemble some in the Vale of Belvoir and Nottinghamshire carved less than ten years earlier. For whatever reason, the English style took vigorous root in America, where it became part of the scene, including type design.

The only other country where external influences affected type design appears to have been Germany, where a healthy tradition of inventive (that is, non-Johnstonian) calligraphy has had an almost subliminal effect on type design, not least because some practising calligraphers have designed types distantly reflecting the personal style of their pen forms. In England, professional lettering craftsmen such as Michael Harvey (who works in all forms of lettering, in all media) likewise bridge the gap between the different disciplines. But that is one designer transposing his own styles: a different form of interaction than the one I have tried to pursue here.

'The historical sense involves a perception,' wrote T S Eliot, 'not only of the pastness of the past, but of its presence; the historical sense compels a man to write not merely with his own generation in his bones, but with a feeling that the whole of literature of Europe from Homer ... has a simultaneous existence.' Similarly, book designers working today should feel the presence of the past; they should be aware of the whole of European printing since Jenson.

Introduction

William Morris wrote of Nicholas Jenson's roman: 'This type I studied with much care, getting it photographed to a big scale, and drawing it over many times before I began designing my own letter.'

So opens the introduction to *An Atlas of Typeforms*, published in 1968. Today the idea of *drawing* letters probably seems bizarre to students and younger designers; but in 1968 it (or Letraset) was still the only realistic way of presenting lettering on your design. Tracing letters off a type specimen sheet, tracing them down, painting them in (continually checking with the original): this laborious process taught you a lot about typeforms and the differences between the styles. Even rubbing down Letraset taught you something. How much real knowledge do you gain today by staring at the computer screen?

Even in 1968 James Sutton and I felt the need for a book drawing attention to the shapes of letters we all take so much for granted. By enlarging selected letters of types then in general use, and relating them to historical examples, we hoped to demonstrate the development of typeforms over the centuries, to provide background understanding to the types we use today, to show how and why the forms changed. As our introduction explained:

This atlas is an attempt to show by illustration, rather than by explaining in words, the main changes in type forms over 500 years of printing. We have enlarged many of the most important types in the history of printing so that their shapes can be seen clearly and compared. We also show, only slightly reduced, an original use of the type, which further demonstrates its qualities; then follow enlarged letters and full alphabets derived from or in the manner of the same historical original.

We have used the broadly chronological headings of Old Face, Transitional, Modern, etc. rather than more sophisticated systems whose virtues are still being debated. Many types today have no very clear ancestry as under modern conditions the use of old type face designs is only

possible after drastic revision; but when learning about types the authors found it helpful to look at the designs of the past in their historical setting. There seemed to be a continuity in the changes in letter forms which made them easier to understand and identify, and comparison with modern faces gave a useful insight into their nature.

This present book omits both the illustrations of somewhat 'distressed' enlargements of historical types, and the books showing these types in use, which made such an impact in the *Atlas*; for we reproduced these huge tomes full size or nearly so, and that necessitated our own book being of monstrous size too, much to the dislike of bookshops, and presenting storage problems to the purchaser as well. But in those days publishers relied on their personal judgement, or hunch; ours barely blinked at a request for a book 405 × 255 mm. Despite the size, or perhaps because of it, the *Atlas* became a classic. Yet it almost immediately became out-of-date; for while the book was splendidly printed by offset, all the types shown were metal, to be consigned to history a mere year or two later and replaced by early filmset types, far inferior both to the metal forms and to today's PostScript types. It is these metal forms that are shown here, for reasons explained earlier. The enlargements still demonstrate what amazing shapes these taken-for-granted symbols are, and which the human mind can turn into sound, thoughts and ideas.

This is emphatically not a type specimen book, and any attempt to use it as such could produce dismaying results, even though most types shown are available in PostScript form. What it sets out to do is relate, clearly and succinctly, the how, why and what of type development. There are far too many new types today; but most merely continue the story along the same lines while being governed by the requirements of new technology. If types are to function they cannot change form too drastically. The changes in the nineteenth and twentieth centuries brought about by the need for powerful display types, in particular the grotesques and the sanserifs, and extravagantly decorated types: such innovations are about as far as one can safely go; although square sanserif forms are acceptable for certain display uses (firms' names) or, especially, architectural situations. Specialist forms – machine readable characters, for instance – are aesthetically displeasing, often difficult to read, and can sensibly only be used outside their designed purpose for limited referential or atmospheric effect.

Letters have negative as well as positive forms: white space within (or outside) the form is important. Looking *into* the letter, so to speak, into that white space, helps us to identify differences in form. The large-scale letters here facilitate this. These symbols can be regarded as fine abstract shapes; they have often been so used in the twentieth century.

Why should twenty-first century designers concern themselves with how letterforms changed, in almost indiscernable ways, over the previous five centuries? What relevance does this knowledge have either to the requirements of today's society or to its typography? The Swiss magazine *Neue Grafik*, published between 1958 and 1965, had 'a policy of reproducing only work which is absolutely contemporary in style'. It demonstrated that New Graphic Design was inherently Swiss, was inevitably 'Constructive', and developed logically from modernism. It was uncompromising in its promotion of Swiss 'hard-edge' design. Yet it contained numerous historical articles, and was criticised by Paul Schuitema, the veteran Dutch survivor from the De Stijl period, for doing so. 'It is not a particularly good thing that people should be interested in what was going on in the Thirties … it has already become part of history. The only possibility is to go on logically from there, from those clear, definite principles.' So why did *Neue Grafik* continue to show those old examples, and why should we bother with them? We need them

because, used creatively, they can enrich our own work.

However different our approach to design may be from that of earlier centuries, its essential ingredient is still the word. The basic construction of letters that form words, without which our society could not operate, always needs to be understood. Too distorted, they become unreadable and meaningless. By studying the changes in historical forms, we can judge how far we can go. It was an enormous leap from the classic types of the eighteenth century to mid-nineteenth century grotesques; yet the skeleton form remained. We need to know why the changes took place, why that basic form is still visible and can still be read even if, at the time of their conception, they were considered ugly.

That is the primary aim of this book; yet knowledge of the history of type has secondary benefits. Most of the types shown here, having been developed from historical models, have period resonances, and these can be exploited to create atmosphere, just as designers of TV costume dramas aim at authentic lettering for their shop fronts. A book of eighteenth-century poetry need not be set in a type of that period, but such an associative effect – even if not consciously registered by the reader – need be no gimmick. Conversely, an otherwise strictly 'hard-edge' modernist design can be enhanced by the anachronistic use – either for display, for the text, or both – of a classic serifed typeface. The designer's job is to create a conduit that conveys ideas, thoughts, knowledge or feelings in the clearest possible way. Over five hundred years of tradition are there to be plundered to this end.

While not the designer's sole means of communication, language and words usually form an important part of their work. The way they are presented adds to the effectiveness of the design. We need not go so far as the Italian Futurists who deconstructed both elements for emotional ends and for more emphatic communication. 'The Futurist,' declared Marinetti, 'will waste no time in

building sentences … my new array of type, this original use of characters, enable me to increase many times the expressive power of words.' The Futurists deployed a wide variety of types, often in the same word. They knew that the typestyle from which words are formed will affect the reader's reaction to those words, add to the effectiveness or meaning of the text, perhaps even to an additional perception of its meaning. Types create an atmosphere, even if subliminally. The Futurists' aims – the creation of individual and personal visual poetry – were quite different from those of the Swiss designers, who chose a type in harmony with their 'anonymous' intellectually ordered designs. Typeforms are some of the most vital tools in any designer's work. The more we can understand them, the more effectively we can use them.

We are so familiar with letters and their shapes, we take so much for granted, give them no thought. Typeforms have developed to such an extent that their origins as pen-formed lettering are completely disguised. Yet that technique has dictated the structure of virtually all type. Even grotesques show vestigial signs of the thicks and thins created by the movement of the pen; the serifs of classic faces are a continuation of the neat way of terminating straight strokes contrived by the pen; the very existence of lowercase letters, a typesetting term derived from the position of drawers in the cabinets in which metal type was stored: they owe their origin to easier-and-quicker-to-form minuscules developed from capitals by monks and others for their manuscripts. So we must treat letters with respect. We are handling history, even if it appears as eye-glazing images on a computer screen. When the Swiss graphic designers of 1950 onwards – illustrated so thoroughly in *Neue Grafik* – used Akzidenz Grotesk or Helvetica as if they were simply powerful abstract shapes, they nevertheless did so with understanding. When they chose to use these richer and less mechanical grotesques derived from nineteenth-century models, rather than the geometric, more 'modern', thoroughly twentieth-century Futura – which might have seemed the obvious and more appropriate type for their rigorous style – they had the knowledge and feeling for a type which countered what might otherwise have been an over-clinical appearance.

Designers often today dismiss the 'Swiss style' and its grids as irrelevant. Yet despite their original invention for and application to the mechanics of letterpress printing, grids still have meaning in the age of computer originated design. And however we design, we still use the same letterforms; a good knowledge of type – its history and its development – is just as important as it ever was. Sensitivity to these shapes, a feeling for the right type in the right place; such basic requirements of one's trade are only acquired by a careful study of these commonplace objects.

This book has two stories. The main one is the story of type; but alongside it, parallel to it for much of the way yet connecting to it from time to time, is a related story of other lettering. By Victorian times the two join, become closely related. The early lettering is carved on buildings of some architectural pretention; but it later appears on humbler buildings and situations, and in wood, or metal, or painted, or in mosaic or ceramic. Type occurs in a context: it is not something that happens in a vacuum, disconnected from its period, its surroundings or contemporaneous events. Regardless of situation or purpose, all lettering tends to move, century by century, along a similar path, taking similar forms at any particular time. The illustrations have been chosen to demonstrate this, and also to depict the wider background in which both type and lettering operate.

If the Romans had not created the roman alphabet, another people would have had to create their own alphabet. But it was the Roman Empire, stretching from North Britain to the Middle East and North Africa, that disseminated the roman form around half the known world and ensured the survival of the alphabet we use today. And it was their descendents, the Renaissance Italians, those born-again Romans – artists and architects, scholars and printers – who refined the alphabet and added the definitive and, on the whole, well-related minuscules. And it was the people of a small north-western island, once a distant part of the Roman Empire, who, 1700 years later, considering themselves the New Romans, felt the need to recreate the spirit of Rome in their buildings. In the twentieth century, Italian fascists looked back again and made serious efforts to echo their Roman heroes with buildings adorned, in the Roman manner, with lettering.

It is notable that it was these self-proclaimed New Romans – fifteenth- and sixteenth-century Italians, eighteenth- and nineteenth-century British, twentieth-century Italian fascists – who, almost uniquely amongst western people, were anxious to incorporate, to integrate, lettering on their buildings. How this debt to the Romans, continually reflected in architecture, marches along with developments in type design, is the story of this book.

Buried among evergreen oaks, perched on a ledge of vertical rock overlooking a gorge, the remote monastery of S Benedetto, outside Subiaco, was where, in 1465, two Germans, Sweynheym and Pannartz, printed the first book produced in Italy. The type was heavy, rather condensed, and expressed roman shapes in gothic dress. The two men soon moved to Rome, 50km to the west, and cut a new type with no gothic characteristics, which became known as 'roman' type. Imperfect, it is yet recognisable as 'our' type. At the same time two German brothers, the da Spiras, working in Venice, initiated the fine series of types that emanated from that city, and which were so crucial in the history of printing.

Italy was the motherland of new learning and the centre of the Renaissance. Venice, the queen of the Adriatic, was mistress of world-wide trade. This combination of culture and commerce attracted to that city many who appreciated that printing would play a major part in both spheres. By 1480 there were over fifty printers at work in Venice; by the turn of the century, 150: an expansion rivalling, in relative terms, that of the internet today. But the bubble did not burst. Even by 1490 Venice had far eclipsed any other city in Europe for its print production and organised distribution. This is the world of Carpaccio, whose paintings convey the bustling international character of the city's trade and culture so vividly.

The manuscript writers used a chisel-ended pen. Moved down the page, this produced a thick stroke; moved across, a thin stroke. These scribes held the pen at an angle. Thus the thickest parts of a round form such as the o take on an oblique stress. The top terminations of vertical strokes were also at an angle; the pull of the pen resulted in a curve, a bracket, where such serifs joined the vertical stroke. But, for stability, the bottom serifs were horizontal, on the base line. These characteristics of lowercase letters are common to all old face types, and can be seen, to a lesser or greater degree, in the caps too.

Lactanius *Opera*. Sweynheym and Pannartz, Subiaco 1465

Cicero *Letters*. Sweynheym and Pannartz, Rome 1470

The oblique stress of rounded forms seems to aid readability, subtly playing against the straight verticals. While the outside form of both the lowercase o and the capital is usually more or less a circle, the inside is oval. Such inside shapes are as important as the outer forms, and were something one becomes aware of when tracing off and drawing letters.

Printing never developed in isolation: the culture behind it was always a powerful influence. The skills of punchcutters, the inventiveness of press builders, the improvements in manufacturing methods which turned that inventiveness into reality, the developments in papermaking, in ink formulation: all contributed. The whole society in which printing was embedded is reflected, century by century, in the overall appearance of the printed result, and in the types which form such a crucial part of it.

The significant stages in the development of the classic serifed roman face can be illustrated by the eight examples opposite. Relating them to their background culture, it can be said that the Venetians supplied Renaissance intellectuals; Kerver, Garamond and their fellows, French noblemen; the Dutch printers, the rising mercantile classes; Caslon, English commerce and down-to-earth commonsense.

A radical change occurred in France, reflecting the haughty brilliance of Louis XIV's court and academic intellectuality of the time. John Baskerville softened this to print, amongst other things, classic texts for the cultured 'Grand Tourers'. Soon his innovations were accentuated by others to create glittering types for English poets and writers, and which reflected a brilliant society and the high technical craftsmanship available. Bodoni continued this trend, perhaps slightly overstepping the mark, with type and books for the sophisticated aristocrat, losing in the process the subtle rhythms of pen forms.

RENAISSANCE SCRIPT. From a Florentine manuscript of 1455

dictu<i>q</i>.Prędimus eum non modo non fecit:fed cum
et poffet rem impedire:fi ut numeraret̃ poftularet tac
affenfus eft qui & locutus honorifice nõ decreuerat fu
ad hos Fauonius acceffit. Quare pro cuiufq̃ natura &
agend<i>s</i>:his q̃ tantũ uolũtate oftéderunt pro fententia
nõ pugnarũt.Curioni uero q̃ de fua<i>y</i> actionũ curfu
Furuius & Lentulus ut debuerũt quafi eo<i>y</i> res eff&:
et laborarũt.Balbi quoq̃ Cornelii operam & fedulitat

parato di ornamenti,& di pompe,& fumptuofi ueftimé
& culto,piu che regio,cum exquifitiffimo exornato p-
néte uenerante,di tenera, & florentiffima ætatula q̃ iu-
:he, cum uirginei allectabuli,& cœlefti , & illuftri afpe-
:cum decentiffimo famulitio obfequiofe tute fe da pati
nte tute le thereutice paftophore,pyrgophore,& le anti
deuano ,cum trophæi di militare decoramenti in hafta

pefle mefle en troupe, ainfi que chacun fe trouuoit.
des perfonnages,& le fon des inftrumens,haultzbois,
& chalemies,eftoient fi grans, qu'il fembloit que l'air
de felicité viuoient les bienheureux en tout foulas & p
& fuyuant les triumphes, parmy les beaux champs
fleurs de toutes les coleurs, odeurs, & faueurs qu'il|e
aromatifantes que toutes les fortes d'efpices que natu

cipere poffent , provincia abieris. Nihil itac
aut antiquius effe duximus *vir Nobiliffime &*
fime, quam fedulo curare, ut tamen opus
communibus typis noftris defcriptum , & f
nomine , materiæque gravitate Te dignum i
fronte Tuum referret nomen. Hoc vero, c
bi fiftimus , effe quis negabit ? Tibi ftrenuior

année, eftant reparti de Breft mieux accompa
de l'Isle de Tabago, au commencement de D
s'approcha de la Place, & la fit attaquer. Il y
confidérable, & on ne doutoit point que le Sié
fement le fecond jour du fiége, la troifiéme b
ba fur le magafin à poudres, y mit le feu, & fit
Vice-Amiral Hollandois, quinze Officiers , &

man and *Italic* are all I have hitherto
ed; if in thefe he has left room for i
ment, it is probably more owing to tha
which divided his attention, than to an
caufe. I honor his merit, and only
derive fome fmall fhare of Reputatio

Or onward, where the rude Carinthian boor
Against the houseless stranger shuts the doo
Or where Campania's plain forsaken lies,
A weary waste, expanding to the skies ;
Where-e'er I roam, whatever realms to see,

Tentaris numeros. Vt melius, quidquid erit, pat
Seu plures hiemes, seu tribuit Iuppiter ultimam
Quae nunc oppositis debilitat pumicibus mare
Tyrrhenum; sapias, vina liques, et spatio brevi
Spem longam reseces. Dum loquimur, fugerit in
Aetas: carpe diem, quam minimum credula post

1470

The finest pre-Aldus typeface was cut in Venice by a Frenchman, Nicholas Jenson. It provides the model for the group of printing types known as venetians. Jenson used his type not only for books on religious matters, but also for classical texts, Latin and Greek, thus anticipating Aldus in catering for a new public of cultured (and leisured) gentlemen. His type has a heaviness, a blackness (perhaps reflecting his reluctance to abandon the gothic) which was much approved of by the likes of William Morris; but it is less congenial to us today. While retaining the overall characteristics, it has usually been lightened for modern use. Even so, it is a little-used form, its idiosyncrasies – especially the oblique bar of the e – being irritating to the modern eye, used to something perhaps a little blander.

CHARACTERISTICS
Gradual change from thick to thin strokes; oblique stress; serifs strong and steeply sloped (those on caps having no brackets, those on lower case almost only brackets). M sometimes has serifs on the inside, e has small eye with oblique bar.

Ludlow Eusebius

RQENbaegn
baegn

ABCDEFGHIJKLMNOPQRSTUVWXYZ
abcdefghijklmnopqrstuvwxyzæœff fiflffifffl
&ÆŒ£1234567890.,:;-!?"()
ABCDEFGHIJKLMNOPQRSTUVWXYZ
abcdefghijklmnopqrstuvwxyzæœfffifflffifffl
&ÆŒ£1234567890.,:;-!?"()

30pt

Ludlow Eusebius. 1924, E F Detterer.
An adaptation of Jenson's roman of 1470, it
has an italic influenced by sixteenth-century
chancery italic calligraphy.

RQENbaegn
baegn

ABCDEFGHIJKLMNOPQRSTUVWXYZ
abcdefghijklmnopqrstuvwxyzæœfiflffffiffl
&ÆŒ£1234567890.,:;-!?"()
ABCDEFGHIJKLMNOPQRSTUVWXYZ
abcdefghijklmnopqrstuvwxyzæœfiflffffiffl
&ÆŒ£1234567890.,:;-!?"()

30pt

Monotype Centaur. 1929, Bruce Rogers. Adapted by Rogers from his private press type of 1915. Derived from the Jenson original of 1470, it is much lighter in weight than true venetians, evoking some of the character of di Giorgio's lettering at Urbino (opposite).

The italic, originally known as Arrighi, was based on Ludovico degli Arrighi's chancery face of 1524.

Ducal Palace, Urbino; courtyard, about 1475. Lettering probably by Francesco di Giorgio. The springtime freshness of the early Renaissance, the dew still on the grass, can be felt in this inscription, just as in Aldus's books. New forms are being searched for, investigated, discovered. In this golden dawn, vision and skill went hand-in-hand. While cutting in stone on this architectural scale allowed greater delicacy and precision than cutting in metal for type, yet we can see here suggestions both of a light form of venetian and a foretaste of Aldus's type. As appropriate for this splendid building as Aldus's type is for his classical texts, the lettering with its inconsequential eccentricities (the G, the serifs of T and A) seems more the work of a poet than a letterer.

1495

Fourteen years after Jenson's death in 1480, a new roman type made its appearance in Venice. It was to become the archetype of all old face types. The Renaissance publisher Aldus Manutius chose Francesco Griffo to design and cut his types; the results reflected perfectly the cultural background of the day: humanist, formal, ungothic. Just as the form of these Italian capitals owes almost everything to Roman carved inscriptions, the lowercase letters have their origins ultimately, if less obviously, in the work of Roman scribes. Their cursives and half-uncials of the third to fifth centuries eventually evolved into the Anglo-Irish half-uncials which Charlemagne's scriptorium transformed into the Carolingian minuscule. Renaissance scribes based their humanistic minuscules upon it (believing it to be the style of the ancients, or Romans); Venetian printers took this form as their model. Initiating a new era in typography, these types epitomised the Renaissance spring. Aldus was a scholar. He rarely if ever printed religious subjects; a man of his times, his books were editions of classical texts: Latin, Italian, Greek. Griffo's types were the perfect medium. Aldus printed them as carefully planned, comfortable pages of readable text, sometimes with woodcut illustrations which were perfectly judged in their weight and colour to match the type. In this world of learning and culture, with its new public of scholars, parsons, schoolmasters, lawyers, doctors, who had emerged from university eager to continue their reading, Aldus was very successful, and thus influential. Northern Europe might continue with its gothic types; but Italy (and France) had finished with them. Aldus's romans showed the way forward.

CHARACTERISTICS
Calligraphic stress: thicks and the triangular bracketted serifs at an oblique angle. Round forms generally oval. Close fitting. Open counters, fairly long ascenders and descenders. Cap height slightly less than ascenders. Crossbar of e high and horizontal.

Monotype Bembo

1501

Griffo's roman types were not his only contribution to printing history. The new reading public wanted books that could be easily carried on walks and travels; many of the existing volumes were of considerable size and weight. So Griffo invented a new, condensed, slanting, space-saving form: the italic, closely derived from calligraphic models. Unfortunately Griffo's italic had serious design faults: in an attempt to imitate quickly-executed handwriting too closely, he created over sixty ligatured letters which, ironically, slowed down the compositors' work considerably. The result is rather cramped and hard to read. Later italics such as those designed by the writing master and printer, Arrighi, are much more successful. They are still narrow, slightly slanting letters; but Arrighi was not concerned with economising on space, so his types are less cramped and more readable. Like Griffo he used roman capitals, also, like Griffo's, shorter than the ascenders. Arrighi's italic forms the basis of many modern versions, which are designed to relate closely to their romans, and are given italic caps (shorter than the ascenders) to match.

In the sixteenth and even the seventeenth centuries whole books were often set in italic, using this as a type independent of any roman. It was Grandjean at the end of the seventeenth century who first provided an italic conceived as a mate for the roman, when he cut his *romain du roi*. Old face italics had often been irregular in slope, but now the slope of the lowercase, and to a large extent the caps too, was regularised, and their cursive serifs gradually gave way to ones that, in moderns, were flat, hairline and horizontal, and with caps the same height as the ascenders. Without creating a mere sloped roman, the aim was to harmonise the italic and roman forms of a type, yet keeping sufficient difference between the two.

CHARACTERISTICS
Lowercase letters of the earlier, old face, italics have decided although irregular slope. Angled semi-cursive serifs, slightly bracketted. Initially, roman caps were used; italic caps introduced 1524. Their slope also irregular, less inclined than lowercase. Cap height less than ascenders.

Italics of transitional and modern types have mechanical regularity of slope. Sharp and often great contrast between thicks and thins. Serifs of transitional caps, ascenders and descenders flat and slightly bracketted. In moderns, they are unbracketted, as are tops of stems of i, m, n, p and u. Thins and serifs hairline. Cap height as ascenders.

Monotype Bembo italic

RQENbaegn
baegn

ABCDEFGHIJKLMNOPQRSTUVWXYZ
abcdefghijklmnopqrstuvwxyzæœfifl
&ÆŒ£1234567890.,;:-!?"'()
ABCDEFGHIJKLMNOPQRSTUVWXYZ
abcdefghijklmnopqrstuvwxyzæœfifl
&ÆŒ£1234567890.,;:-!?"'()

30pt PostScript Poliphilus and Blado Italic

Monotype Poliphilus. 1923.
A facsimile revival of Aldus's roman of 1499, retaining all the original irregularities. It was copied from pages showing the type heavier and a little worn; but this unintentionally gives it a markedly individual character, and also one that survives digitisation better than many hot metal types. The italic, originally known as Blado italic, was based on letters used by Antonio Blado, printer to the Vatican, and designed by Arrighi in 1526. In hot metal, the largest size of Poliphilus (the roman) was 16pt. It is shown here, together with the italic, in its digitised form.

RQENbaegn
R *baegn*

ABCDEFGHIJKLMNOPQRSTUVWXYZ
abcdefghijklmnopqrstuvwxyzæœfffiflffiffl
&ÆŒ£1234567890.,;:-!?"()
ABCDEFGHIJKLMNOPQRSTUVWXYZ
abcdefghijklmnopqrstuvwxyzæœfffiflffiffl
&ÆŒ£1234567890.,;:-!?"()

30pt

Monotype Bembo. 1929.
Derived from Aldus's *De Aetna* roman of 1495, with the capitals lightened and regularised. The long-legged R of the original design goes back to Roman inscriptions and also reappears in Renaissance work. In these slightly letterspaced inscriptions it created no problems; but in type, followed by lowercase letters or in un-letterspaced lines of caps, it resulted in displeasing spacing, kicking the next letter away. Consequently, Monotype brought out an alternative short-legged R, less elegant but more practical.

   The italic is from revised chancery types used and probably designed by Giovantonio Tagliente.

Obelisk in Piazza San Giovanni in Latero, Rome, 1588. Lettering designed by Luca Horfei, cut by Matheo di Meli.
The excitement of young discovery seen at Urbino has now, over a hundred years later, matured into a unified, fully worked-out set of letters. There is nothing inconsequential about this lettering. Similarly, Garamond took the earlier Italian types and refined them. While Francesco di Giorgio at Urbino lacked no skills, advances in the skills of typecutting are clearly evident in Garamond's work. We may sometimes regret the loss of early exuberance and fun as it grows into mature perfection, and the story of lettering is not all gain; yet Horfei's design here is stately and highly civilised, in the same way that the work of Garamond (and his fellows) was.

Horfei's letters are in general remarkably similar to Monotype's Bembo. The most noticeable differences are that Horfei's A has a pointed top, whereas it is cut off in Bembo, and the lower curve of his P does not join the stem.

1540

During the second quarter of the sixteenth century the leadership in typographic design passed to France. Pages of type became lighter, and borders of printed flowers and decorative headbands became more common, although generally still used sparingly. The Aldine letter was given a new grace and assurance, the fit of the letters improved, the balance between capitals, lowercase and italic carefully harmonised. This new roman (and its italic) was primarily the work of Claude Garamond. Originally based on Griffo's roman and Arrighi's italic, he later developed both forms technically and aesthetically. A page of his unleaded, unparagraphed text is elegant, distinguished and evenly textured. Such grandeur was much at home in the libraries of the contemporaneous Loire chateaux. Both buildings and books are fundamentally traditional, incorporating Renaissance ideas imported from Italy. But to the modern eye, the pages look a daunting read, more so than those of Aldus. The type itself, however, is much advanced.

CHARACTERISTICS
Based on Italian types. Balance of capitals, lowercase and italic more fully harmonised. Gradual smooth transition from stem to serif. More rounded triangular serifs, generally shorter and blunter.

Linotype Granjon

RQEN baegn
baegn

ABCDEFGHIJKLMNOPQRSTUVWXYZ
abcdefghijklmnopqrstuvwxyzæœffffiflffiffl
&ÆŒ£1234567890.,;:-!?"()
ABCDEFGHIJKLMNOPQRSTUVWXYZ
abcdefghijklmnopqrstuvwxyzæœfffiflffiffl
& ÆŒ£1234567890.,;:-!?"()

30pt

Monotype Garamond. 1922.
The first type revived by Monotype under Morison, it was based on punches from the Imprimerie Royale, then attributed to Garamond but now known to have been cut by Jannon about 1620. These forms, developed from Garamond's, were lighter and more open than his. The italic is from a fount of Granjon, about the middle of the sixteenth century.

RQENbaegn
baegn

ABCDEFGHIJKLMNOPQRSTUVWXYZ
abcdefghijklmnopqrstuvwxyzæœflfifffffiffl
&ÆŒ1234567890.,;:-!?"()
ABCDEFGHIJKLMNOPQRSTUVWXYZ
abcdefghijklmnopqrstuvwxyzæœflfifffffiffl
&ÆŒ1234567890.,;:-!?"()

24D roman and 20D italic

Deberny & Peignot Garamond. 1912-28.
George and Charles Peignot.
Closely resembles the original Garamond type
of 1532. The italic was not brought out larger
than 20D, shown here with 24D roman.

RQENbaegn
baegn

ABCDEFGHIJKLMNOPQRSTUVWXYZ
abcdefghijklmnopqrstuvwxyz
&£1234567890.,;:-!?"()

ABCDEFGHIJKLMNOPQRSTUVWXYZ
abcdefghijklmnopqrstuvwxyzæœfiflffffiffl
&ÆŒ£1234567890.,;:-!?"( )

30pt roman and 14pt italic

Linotype Granjon. Supervised by G W Jones,
1928-31.
Based on a sixteenth-century Paris book
perhaps printed by Garamond, and despite its
name has been called the best reproduction of
a Garamond type today. The italic was
produced no larger than 14pt.

1670

The types of Garamond and his follower Granjon were so widely admired and successful they were exported throughout Europe. They were much used in seventeenth-century Netherlands, until the Dutch cut their own robust workaday versions. Christopher van Dijk and the Voskens family produced some of the finest. The stolid sturdy letters were very similar to French models, although their shorter ascenders and descenders resulted in a loss of elegance; yet pages set in these types had considerable presence, the Dutch burghers of Rembrandt's paintings in typographic dress.

The Frenchman Christopher Plantin moved in 1548 to Antwerp, then Europe's leading centre of publishing. Not a punchcutter himself, he became one of the most notable printers in Europe, with a vast stock of types cut by others.

CHARACTERISTICS
Somewhat weightier than French old face, with bigger body to lowercase letters. Stress and serifs basically as previous old faces. Sprightly and sometimes irregular italic, but more regular than the French.

Monotype Van Dijck

Stapleford Park, Leicestershire, 1633. What are we to make of this lettering? It is certainly more different from earlier forms than Dutch types are from Garamond's. Yet the wholly changed society suggested here, with very different concerns from those of Venetian scholars or French noblemen, is similarly reflected in the worldly types of Dutch printers, and their public. This original lettering has a faintly calligraphic character and a slightly provincial feel, far removed from Italian sensitivity or French sophistication. The strong contrast between thicks and thins is something which became increasingly evident in the development of Dutch types, perhaps reflecting increasing skill in punchcutting.

The sometimes eccentric proportions and irregular spacing do not make this a serene inscription. But the satisfyingly three-dimensional relief form gives it appropriate authority, even assertiveness.

RQENbaegn
baegn

ABCDEFGHIJKLMNOPQRSTUVWXYZ
abcdefghijklmnopqrstuvwxyzæœffffifflffiffl
&ÆŒ£1234567890.,;:-!?"()
ABCDEFGHIJKLMNOPQRSTUVWXYZ
abcdefghijklmnopqrstuvwxyzæœfiflfffffiffl
& ÆŒ£1234567890.,:;-!?"()

30pt

Monotype Plantin. 1913, F H Pierpoint.
From a Granjon face, used by the successors
of Christopher Plantin of Antwerp, working
during the sixteenth century. The modern
type is the first to be designed for art paper,
the sturdier letters making up for the lack of
ink squash. With an unusually large x-height
for the time, it was a pioneer attempt at
making a type economical in paper.

RQENbaegn

baegn

ABCDEFGHIJKLMNOPQRSTUVWXYZ
abcdefghijklmnopqrstuvwxyzæœfiflffffiffl
&ÆŒ£1234567890.,:;-!?"'()

ABCDEFGHIJKLMNOPQRSTUVWXYZ
abcdefghijklmnopqrstuvwxyzæœfiflffffiffl
&ÆŒ£1234567890.,:;-!?"'()

30pt

Monotype Van Dijck. 1935, with the assistance
of Van Krimpen.
From a roman appearing in an Amsterdam
edition of Ovid, printed in 1671, but not
definitely by Van Dijck himself.

RQENbaegn
baegn

ABCDEFGHIJKLMNOPQRSTUVWXYZ
abcdefghijklmnopqrstuvwxyzæœfifl
&ÆŒ£1234567890.,;:-!?()
ABCDEFGHIJKLMNOPQRSTUVWXYZ
abcdefghijklmnopqrstuvwxyzæœfifl
&ÆŒ£1234567890.,;:-!?()

30pt PostScript Ehrhardt

Monotype Ehrhardt. 1938.
A regularised version of a type by Nicholas
Kis of 1672. Kis was a Hungarian punchcutter
working in Amsterdam.

1725

William Caslon's types of 1725 and onwards are classified as Dutch old face, and they exhibit the same general characteristics. However, he is important because he initiated a long line of fine punchcutters, which ended British printers' reliance on Dutch types. For almost a hundred years, the design and execution of printing in Britain equalled anywhere in the world. And despite the innovative achievements and, to our eyes today, the finer types, of John Baskerville, Caslon remained the roman of choice for most printers in the country until well into the nineteenth century. They were no better than their Dutch models, but English printers could now use English types, and they did so in an unpretentious, practical but not inelegant way. They felt comfortable with these well-cut forms and their decent fit. It was like wearing a favourite old suit.

Caslon 'Englished' Dutch types, a development later accentuated by Baskerville, and for fifty years English and Scottish type designers took the lead. In other fields, English lettering was even more transforming, and for longer.

OPPOSITE
Adlington Hall, Cheshire; south wing, 1757. The first half of the eighteenth century was a defining period for English culture: it was the time English and Scottish aristocrats, gentry, scholars, architects and artists were rediscovering ancient Rome. The ruins seemed to release the imagination of these new Romans, allowing it to spread out in ever-widening circles.

The portico of this building, an Englishman's evocation of Rome filtered through the Italian Renaissance, was possibly designed by Charles Legh himself. Yet the lettering, while correctly positioned on the pediment, has no resemblance to any Roman or Italian inscription. Not incised but, unusually, in relief, it shows the confidence of these self-proclaimed successors to the Romans. That curly-legged unItalian R, already hesitantly used at Stapleford Park, was to become a recurring feature of the English style in both lettering and type.

In the same year as this inscription, Baskerville produced one of his greatest books, the *Works of Virgil*. Yet the lettering here is like neither Caslon's types nor Baskerville's. Caslon looked back to Dutch models; this inscription seems a foretaste of much that was to come. With its strong thins and blunt serifs, it is almost a clarendon, while the letters of generally even width seem to anticipate the proportions of a Victorian grotesque.

Although differing in many respects from Caslon's designs, this inscription, like those types, heralds the independent ways English letterforms were to take.

Monotype Caslon

RQENbaegn
baegn

ABCDEFGHIJKLMNOPQRSTUVWXYZ
abcdefghijklmnopqrstuvwxyzæœefffiflffiffl
&ÆŒ£1234567890.,;:-!?"()
ABCDEFGHIJKLMNOPQRSTUVWXYZ
abcdefghijklmnopqrstuvwxyzæœefffiflffiffl
&ÆŒ£1234567890.,;:-!?"()

30pt

Monotype Caslon. 1915.
An accurate recutting of revived Caslon types.

RQENbaegn
baegn

ABCDEFGHIJKLMNOPQRSTUVWXY
abcdefghijklmnopqrstuvwxyzæœfffiflſt
&ÆŒ1234567890.,;:-!?'„()
ABCDEFGHIJKLMNOPQRSTUVWXYZ
abcdefghijklmnopqrstuvwxyzæœfiflſt
&ÆŒ1234567890.,;:-!?'„()

28D

Haas Caslon. Larger sizes cut in 1944.
Caslon's original matrices were used for
smaller sizes of both roman and italic.

ABCDEFGHIJKLMNOPQRSTUVWXYZ
abcdefghijklmnopqrstuvwxyzæœffffifl
&ÆŒ1234567890.,-:;!?'(),,""»«/[]§*

28D Stempel Janson

St Martin in the Fields, London, 1726. Although the wayward Stapleford Park inscription contradicts this, in general both lettering and type were becoming sharper, with more contrast between thicks and thins and more abrupt changes between them. Stempel's Janson, taken from the original matrices of about 1690, shows this, and the inscription on St Martin is similar in many ways, while also reflecting characteristics of the *romain du roi*: elongated unbracketted serifs, a vertical stress, a curly-legged R. Like many British architects of the time, James Gibbs was enthusiastic about Italian and Roman ideas; he was in Rome from 1703 to 1709, and on this building at least signed himself JACOBO GIBBS, ARCHITECTO. But while the inscription attempts to be fashionable, it is not especially successful: a somewhat chilly addition to this handsome building. The proportions of the letters are a little uneven, as is the spacing. The serifs of the S are unlike anything in type.

Stempel's Janson is usually classified as Dutch old face; but it is so sharply cut, with delicate thins fairly abruptly merging into the thicks, and a near-vertical stress, it is almost a transitional. It demonstrates the direction in which type design is moving – unconsciously towards moderns. The lettering on St Martin is on the same journey.

1700

Printing, like alchemy, attempts to turn base metal (type) into gold, or knowledge; it also prolongs life indefinitely, in the form of books. Unlike alchemy, it is always moving on. A far-reaching development was initiated in France when the Academy decided upon a mathematically-drawn alphabet, the *romain du roi*. Intended exclusively for the Imprimerie Royale, its frigid form, the product of theoreticians and committees (who also invented a point system), it was quietly softened by the punchcutter Philippe Grandjean. It defied the influence of the pen which had lain almost invisibly behind all type design since Nicholas Jenson and earlier, by emphasising a verticality in the strokes, and making the serifs flat and unbracketted. Because the type was a construct of theory, caps were made the same height as ascenders. They therefore jump out of the page. Ever since Jenson, printers and their typecutters had been more subtle, reducing the cap height to avoid this.

The *romain du roi* was theoretically exclusive to the Imprimerie Royale. Despite – or perhaps because of – the committee that designed it, it is not a very successful typeform. It reflects the arrogance of the court of the time, Louis XIV's, which was contemptuously dismissed by Tobias Smollett as 'an ostentation of fastidious pomp, a prodigality of expence, an affectation of munificence, an insolence of ambition and a haughty reserve of deportment.' (Louis was busily building Versailles at the time.)

The characteristics of the *romain du roi* influenced Fleischman's designs of 1730 and those of P-S Fournier from 1742, designs which led to the moderns of Didot (from 1784) and Bodoni. All this was another world from that of trade, commerce and industry in which Caslon, a down-to-earth tradesman and craftsman, operated. His legacy was picked up by Baskerville, who largely ignored the continental extremes to create a more English form.

CHARACTERISTICS
Strong vertical emphasis, fairly abrupt change from thicks to thins. Flat unbracketted serifs, although tops of some lowercase letters angled. Caps and ascenders of equal height.

Monotype Fournier

RQENbaegn
baegn

ABCDEFGHIJKLMNOPQRSTUVWXYZ
abcdefghijklmnopqrstuvwxyzæœfiflffffiffl
&ÆŒ£1234567890.,:;-!?"'()

ABCDEFGHIJKLMNOPQRSTUVWXYZ
abcdefghijklmnopqrstuvwxyzæœfiflffffiffl
&ÆŒ£1234567890.,:;-!?"'()

30pt roman and 18pt italic

Monotype Fournier. 1925
A facsimile of one of Fournier's text types (St Augustin Ordinaire) in his *Manuel Typographique* of 1764. During the development of the Monotype version, two designs were experimentally cut; by mistake, the wrong one was chosen for production. The digitised Monotype version, in which this book is set, has much improved the design, notably by reducing the height of the caps. The Linotype version retains the caps of ascender height.

1750

A far more satisfactory and sympathetic type than the *romain du roi* was designed in 1754 by John Baskerville. A Birmingham japanner, writing master and lettercarver, many tombstones in the South Midlands betray, if not his hand, at least his influence. Quite late in life (he was fifty) he exploited his acquired skills (even his work as a japanner, formulating the glossy black lacquer, gave him expertise in ink making), plus a native inventiveness, to set up as a printer, producing a series of books which have few rivals in the whole history of printing. A perfectionist, he would run an edition of 2000 to get 1500 copies of even colour.

His was a type of great distinction, created in an age of self-complacency: 'self-poised, self-judged and self-approved … of individual initiative … of creative vigour'. Writing masters were now holding their pens more vertically, creating forms with a generally vertical stress. Unlike the theoreticians who designed the *romain du roi*, Baskerville based his types on this living pen form. Generously proportioned, it had the gravity and serenity of Bath terraces, the elegance and craftsmanship of Hepplewhite or Chippendale. Its restraint allowed it to be used for work as varied as bibles, the classics, poetry, essays or books on angling. Unobtrusive, it sits happily on the page and is notably readable. Baskerville used it in a new open style with good leading and wide margins, making earlier classics look congested. His letter-spaced (sometimes too much so) cap headings have a style, an authority, not seen before; the typographic equivalent of those Bath terraces. His subheads or running heads in italic caps, with their occasional swash letter, have unusual cohesion.

Although he was commercially unsuccessful, his type and his books had a decisive impact on the course of printing throughout Europe and America.

CHARACTERISTICS
Generously proportioned. Round letters approaching circular. Softer forms than early transitional, but more contrast between thicks and thins than in old face designs. Generally vertical stress. Rounded serifs slightly angled, slightly bracketted. Lower bowl of g not fully enclosed. Caps shorter than ascenders.

Monotype Baskerville

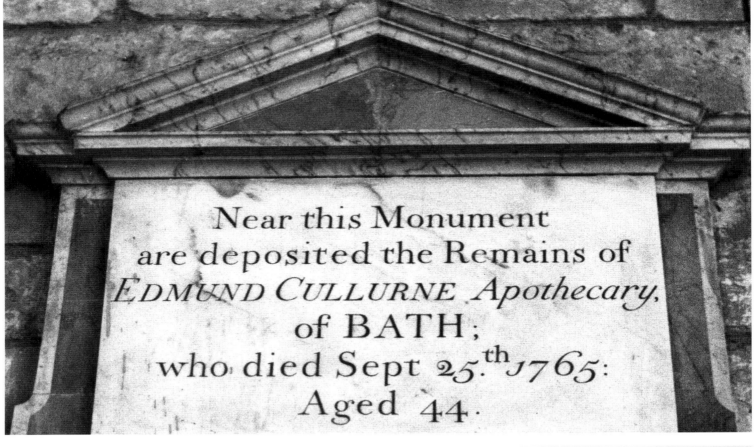

Malmesbury Abbey, Wiltshire.
These two monuments are clearly by the same lettercutter. Despite the date, they have traces of what in type would be called late transitional, with sharp contrasts between thicks and thins; but serifs are still angled. The italic figures are quite Baskerville-like in their verve, and the g has the open lower bowl so characteristic of his type. Inscriptional lettering is moving ever-closer to type; possibly both have a common ancestry in the work of the writing masters of the time. The English vernacular letter is now beginning its long and fruitful journey. In type, it dies out around 1810, becoming subsumed in more dramatic form as Victorian display types bustled in; but in other categories of lettering it continued, in debased form, until about 1980.

RQENbaegn
baegn

ABCDEFGHIJKLMNOPQRSTUVWXYZ
abcdefghijklmnopqrstuvwxyzæœfffifflffiffl
&ÆŒ£1234567890.,;:-!?"'()
ABCDEFGHIJKLMNOPQRSTUVWXYZ
abcdefghijklmnopqrstuvwxyzæœfffifflffiffl
&ÆŒ£1234567890.,;:-!?"'()

30pt

Monotype Baskerville. 1923.
A regularised version of the 1757 Virgil Great
Primer fount. It is difficult to believe, today,
that Baskerville's types were never popular
until Monotype's design was brought out.

RQEN baegn

baegn

ABCDEFGHIJKLMNOPQRSTUVWXYZ
abcdefghijklmnopqrstuvwxyzœflfifffffiffl
&Œ1234567890.,;:-!?"()
ABCDEFGHI JKLMNOPQRSTUVWXYZ
abcdefghijklmnopqrstuvwxyzœflfifffffiffl
Œ1234567890.,;:-!?"()

30D roman and 24D italic

Deberny & Peignot Baskerville.
Actually cast from matrices made from
Baskerville's punches; so this is the original
type. The largest size of italic was 24D.

1780

Baskerville's revolutionary letter design was accentuated by William Martin and Richard Austin at the end of the century, their types showing more contrast of thicks and thins, with the vertical stress further emphasised. This was Baskerville dressed up as Beau Brummell, parading past the more flighty Regency buildings. To an extent abandoning the writing master/lettercarver influence, the new style is very much the product of the engraving tool: appropriate for the books now being illustrated by engravings in wood or copper.

The earlier types of this group such as Fry's Baskerville were rounder in form than those that appeared later. These became progressively more condensed as their verticality was emphasised by more abrupt changes between thick strokes and thin. They eventually became virtually indistinguishable from the style that followed them, the modern.

CHARACTERISTICS
Sharper, more contrasting forms than classic transitional. Vertical stress, giving letters generally a condensed appearance. Horizontal bracketted serifs, tapered and pointed. Caps same height as ascenders.

ATF Bulmer

The *grateful* Inhabitants
To GEORGE THE THIRD
On His entering the 50th Year
Of His REIGN.

RQEN baegn
baegn

ABCDEFGHIJKLMNOPQRSTUVWXYZ
abcdefghijklmnopqrstuvwxyzæœfiflffffiffl
&ÆŒ£1234567890.,:;-!?''()
ABCDEFGHIJKLMNOPQRSTUVWXYZ
abcdefghijklmnopqrstuvwxyzæœfiflffffiffl
&ÆŒ£1234567890.,:;-!?''( )

30pt

OPPOSITE
Weymouth, Dorset, 1810.
There are subtle developments here from the previous carved example. Serifs are horizontal, a sharper change from thicks to thins results in a more vertical stress, the figures are lining, not non-lining, the lower bowl of the g is closed. All these features are found also in late transitional type. The characteristically English curly-legged R is repeated, to be continued in all English forms until (and often including) sanserifs and grotesques. But the rather expanded lettering here is not echoed in type, where letters tend to become a little narrower than before.

Below the photograph the inscription is shown set in PostScript Bell. The sizes of this, the inscription and the 30pt metal version on this page have been made approximately the same. The type has more perfect form; but allowing for its slightly expanded letters the carved form shows a marked family resemblance to the late transitional typeface of 22 years earlier.

Monotype Bell. 1931.
A facsimile copy from punches cut in 1788 by Richard Austin for John Bell which, together with the matrices, had descended to Stephenson Blake.

RQENbaegn

ABCDEFGHIJKLMNOPQRSTUVWXYZ
abcdefghijklmnopqrstuvwxyzfffifflfffiffl
&£1234567890.,;:-!?"

30pt

Stephenson Blake Fry's Baskerville. 1913.
Originally cut by Isaac Moore for Dr Fry in
1769. The 30pt and larger sizes were engraved
and cut by Stephenson Blake. It has much in
common with late transitional types such as
Bell, with greater contrast between thicks and
thins than in the original Baskerville.

RQEN baegn
baegn

ABCDEFGHIJKLMNOPQRSTUVWXYZ
abcdefghijklmnopqrstuvwxyzfifffflffiffl
&$1234567890.,-:;!?""

ABCDEGFHIJKLMNOPQRSTUVWXYZ
abcdefghijklmnopqrstuvwxyzfifffflfflffi
&$1234567890.,-:;!?""

30pt

ATF Bulmer. 1928, M F Benton.
From original cuttings by William Martin
for William Bulmer of the Shakespeare Press,
about 1790. The new design is a little nearer
a modern face than the original. Monotype
brought out a version in 1936, but in 11pt and
12pt only; this range of sizes was later
extended.

RQENbaegn

baegn

ABCDEFGHIJKLMNOPQRSTUVWXYZ
abcdefghijklmnopqrstuvwxyzæœfiflffffiffl
&ÆŒ£1234567890.,:;-!?''()
ABCDEFGHIJKLMNOPQRSTUVWXYZ
abcdefghijklmnopqrstuvwxyzæœfiflffffiffl
&ÆŒ£1234567890.,:;-!?''()

30pt

Monotype Scotch Roman. 1920.
This was produced for the printers R & R
Clark, and is an accurate recutting of the
Miller & Richard type of 1810.

The Old Anchor Inn, Abingdon, Berkshire. This splendid V-cut form links late transitional types, Scotch Roman for instance, with English moderns such as Modern No 20. Like them, but unlike continental moderns (Bodoni, Didot, Walbaum) it has not only looped or curly bottom serifs, but looped top serifs too. This gives a dancing rhythm that the others lack.

Generally speaking, the modern is not much favoured for architectural or even vernacular use. It can be seen in France, in Paris and elsewhere, on enamelled street nameplaces in an almost fatform face; and notably throughout Venice in stencilled letters on the wall, performing the same service. It is not a form suited to large-scale architectural use: the abrupt differences between thicks and thins mitigate against this.

1784

Although unappreciated at home, and his types somewhat travestied, John Baskerville's typography was much admired in continental Europe and America. His pared-down page design greatly influenced French, German and Italian printers, although they all developed types which were more closely derived from the *romain du roi* and were almost a mockery of Baskerville's cautious improvements. Fine hairlines, abrupt changes from thick to thin, horizontal unbracketted serifs which were also hairline thin: none of this helped the reader. The letters themselves were beautifully designed if chilly; sophisticated and novel. G B Bodoni in particular was a consummate craftsman: his type design, his layouts (eliminating everything except type and the occasional minimal decoration) and his printing were all of the highest standard.

The classic authors were presented in the grand manner.

Aristocratic, neo-classical, dignified, almost pompous, his types and other moderns need to be well leaded or their strong verticality binds the lines together, fighting the eye's attempt to read horizontally. When these types were used, not by perfectionist craftsmen but in inferior form by general printers, with little or no leading and wide word spacing, the printing industry entered one of its longest and most dismal episodes. Not until William Morris, living his medieval dream, founded the Kelmscott Press in 1891, were standards revived; although his books, with their mannered heavy type and overwhelming decoration, are not something we wish to emulate today. Bizarrely, the books of both Morris and Bodoni were luxury items.

CHARACTERISTICS
Strong contrast between thicks and hairline thins, giving extreme vertical stress. Horizontal unbracketted serifs. Caps same height as ascenders.

Ludwig & Mayer Firmin Didot

RQEN baegn
baegn

ABCDEFGHIJKLMNOPQRSTUVWXYZ
abcdefghijklmnopqrstuvwxyzæœffffifl
&ÆŒ£1234567890.,;:-!?''()

ABCDEFGHIJKLMNOPQRSTUVWXYZ
abcdefghijklmnopqrstuvwxyzæœffffifl
&ÆŒ£1234567890.,;:-!?''()

30pt

Bauer Bodoni. 1926, Heinrich Jost.
Based on a type in Bodoni's *Manuale
Tipografico* of 1818. This contains 285
alphabets, all variations on modern-face,
although not all of them were designed by
him. In his typography he would use slight
variations of weight and size to achieve his
aims. Bauer's type is based on one of the more
delicate versions.

RQENbaegn

baegn

ABCDEFGHIJKLMNOPQRSTUVWXYZ
abcdefghijklmnopqrstuvwxyzæœfffiflfffiffl
&ÆŒ£1234567890.,;:-!?"'()
ABCDEFGHIJKLMNOPQRSTUVWXYZ
abcdefghijklmnopqrstuvwxyzæœfffifffiffl
ÆŒ&£1234567890.,;:-!?"'()

30pt

Monotype Bodoni. 1921.
Based on a type in *Manuale Tipografico*. The
form is similar to Bauer's version, but bolder.
Monotype also produced a somewhat lighter
version, Bodoni Book, in text sizes only.

RQENbaegn
baegn

ABCDEFGHIJKLMNOPQRSTUVWXYZ
abcdefghijklmnopqrstuvwxyzæœffffififlft
&ÆŒ£1234567890.,;:-!?'"""()
ABCDEFGHIJKLMNOPQRSTUVWXYZ
abcdefghijklmnopqrstuvwxyzæœ
&ÆŒ1234567890.,;:-!?'"""()

30pt

Ludwig & Mayer Firmin Didot.
Closely follows the originals of Firmin Didot
types from 1784 onwards. It was recut from
eighteenth-century drawings which survive,
using also printed specimens as references.
Deberny & Peignot held the original punches.

RQENbaegn

baegn

ABCDEFGHIJKLMNOPQRSTUVWXYZ
abcdefghijklmnopqrstuvwxyzæœffffifl
&ÆOE£1234567890.,;:-!?"()
ABCDEFGHIJKLMNOPQRSTUVWXYZ
abcdefghijklmnopqrstuvwxyzæœffffifl
&ÆOE£1234567890.,;:-!?"()

30D

Berthold Walbaum.
Cast from the original matrices of Justus
Erich Walbaum, about 1800, which were
acquired by Berthold in 1919.

RQENbaegn
baegn

ABCDEFGHIJKLMNOPQRSTUVWXYZ
abcdefghijklmnopqrstuvwxyzfffififlffiffl
&£1234567890.,;:-!?""

ABCDEFGHIJKLMNOPQRSTUVWXYZ
abcdefghijklmnopqrstuvwxyzæœfffififlffiffl
&ÆŒ£1234567890.,;:-!?""()

30pt

Stephenson Blake Modern 20.
Derived from a number of faces, mostly cut
by Stephenson Blake in the late nineteenth
century.

1810

The moderns, which could be unsatisfactory text types, were the basis of the new kind of letter required by a changed society. The men of the Industrial Revolution demanded punchy display alphabets for jobbing work. The obvious solution was to take the currently fashionable moderns and thicken them up. The resulting fatfaces, first issued in 1810, were visually unexpectedly successful: they certainly attracted attention, and the shapes formed are extremely interesting as abstract designs. The same applies to the later display faces: egyptians, clarendons, grotesques. Used forcefully, even brutally, these types are difficult to ignore. Looking *into* the letters, as well as at their outer form, provides a new experience, a new appreciation of these amazing symbols we call letters. For all their power, the best are subtly designed with a confidence and flair that can be found in the engineering of the day. Clarendons and egyptians were actually used on that engineering: their sturdy cast forms could almost have been designed by the same engineers. The basic form of all these types can survive almost wilful distortion.

FATFACE CHARACTERISTICS
Despite their extreme, almost gross forms, they are subtly designed. Junctions between thicks and thins sometimes merged. Curves, especially the terminations of strokes, are vital and sprightly. Thick strokes are vertical, serifs horizontal hairlines. Much variation in detail: some alphabets have very short ascenders and descenders.

Monotype Falstaff

Clonmel, Co Tipperary: cast iron and painted plaque.

While fatfaces are adaptable to many media – signwriting, carving, ceramics – they are less amenable to casting because of the delicacy of their thins. Yet here is an extreme example, so fat that counters almost disappear. The merging junctions of curved forms relate it more closely to the rich shapes of Falstaff than to the slightly crude Bodoni ultrabold.

RQENbae
baegn gn

ABCDEFGHIJKLMNO
PQRSTUVWXYZ
abcdefghijklmnopqrstuvwxyzæœ
fiflffffiffl&ÆŒ£1234567890.,;:-!?""()
ABCDEFGHIJKLMNOPQRSTU
VWXYZabcdefghijklmnopqrs
tuvwxyzæœfiflffffiffl&
ÆŒ£1234567890.,;:-!?""()

30pt

Monotype Bodoni ultrabold. 1936.
A fatface version of Monotype's Bodoni. The
junctions of thick and thin strokes are abrupt.

RQENbae
baegn gn

ABCDEFGHIJKLMNOPQRS
TUVWXYZabcdefghijklmnop
qrstuvwxyzæœ ff ffi fl ffffffl
&ÆŒ£1234567890.,;:-!?""'()
ABCDEFGHIJKLMNOPQRS
TUVWXYZabcdefghijklmnop
qrstuvwxyzæœfiflffffffiffl
&ÆŒ£1234567890.,;:-!?""'()

30D on 36pt

Monotype Falstaff. 1935.
Here the junctions of thicks and thins merge,
resulting in less harsh shapes. Nearer to the
Victorian form than Bodoni ultrabold.

RQEN

baegn

ABCDEFGHIJKLMNOPQRS
TUVWXYZ·AMNVW
abcdefghijklmnopqrstuvwxyz
œæ&ŒÆ£1234567890,.:;-!?'(

30pt

Stephenson Blake Thorowgood italic.
Revived from matrices of 1810 (perhaps
those of Thorne), and is in its original form.
A roman was revived in 1953, but withdrawn
due to lack of demand. The italic has even
richer forms than Falstaff, with curved tops
and bottoms to 'vertical' strokes.

1815

Late eighteenth- and early nineteenth-century Englishmen, owning half the world, felt themselves to be the new Romans. On their travels they had noticed that Roman buildings were adorned with lettering; so, they thought, we must put lettering on our neo-classical buildings. Their preferred architectural influence was not Roman but Greek; but Greek buildings had no lettering, so they had to imagine a suitable form. They believed the more barbaric this was, the more Greek it would be. The fashion was for the Noble Savage and rugged antiquity (as they thought of it). So they concluded that letters without serifs would be just the ticket. Alternatively, slab serifs – another primitive shape – could be added to such a form. The result can be seen in a one-word heading of an 1808 illustration by Humphrey Repton; but it appears more significantly in the headings (not at all barbaric) to the plates in *The Architectural Antiquities of Rome*, published in 1822 to disseminate more accurate ideas of Roman architecture. This became an important source book for English architects, who must have noted that lettering … eventually.

For, despite the theories of the intelligentsia, the form seems to have made its first serious appearance, in caps only, in an 1815 type specimen book from Figgins, where it was called, significantly, Antique. As the first really original design for the new age, it was welcomed enthusiastically by commerce and its handmaiden, printing. Strangely, it was seemingly never used on major buildings until the mid-nineteenth century. Yet it began to make frequent early appearances on humbler buildings such as pubs and chapels. The form is splendidly architectural, the most so of all letterforms. But it also packed a sledgehammer punch much appreciated by advertisers and jobbing printers. Later versions such as Rockwell were less colourful.

CHARACTERISTICS
Often little or no weight difference between strokes normally thick or thin, although bolder weights force greater variations. Slab, rectangular serifs, no bracketting. Letter widths more regular than in classic text types. Weight ranges from ultra bold to thin. Successfully translates into condensed or very expanded forms.

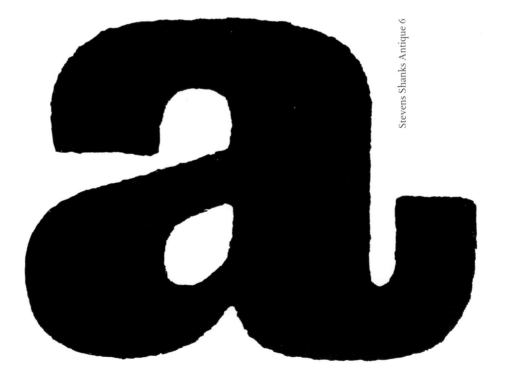

Stevens Shanks Antique 6

Great Torrington, Devon.
Despite the theories of the intelligentsia, busily considering a correct form of lettering for their neo-classical buildings, egyptians were first seen as type; although, as I have said, it had made an insignificant appearance in an engraving of 1808. Be that as it may, it was a style that was in the air, and on this chapel it demonstrates what presence it has, even on such a small scale as this. The rich shapes are given even more impact by the relief form, set against the simple façade. The thick strokes could hardly be bolder without the letters becoming completely solid. It closely resembles Antique No 6; yet that did not appear until about 1860.

Pharmaceutical Society building, Bloomsbury, London. Lettering 1860.

A politer form of egyptian, equally effective, is this regularly proportioned, well-spaced V-cut letter. The R has an unusual straight serifless leg which is not quite in character. Of even weight throughout, Os and Cs are perfect circles. It has much more in common with the later, more geometric types such as Rockwell (1934) than it has with the richer Victorian styles; yet here, as an architectural element, it is particularly successful, as appropriate for this serious building (remodelled by John Nash in the late eighteenth century, but with top storey and lettering added in 1860) as the previous example is for the simple Great Torrington chapel.

RQENbae gn

ABCDEFGHIJKLMNO
PQRSTUVWXYZ
abcdefghijklmnopqrstuv
wxyzæœfififlffffiffl&ÆŒ
£1234567890,;:.-'!?

ABCDEFGHIJKLMNOPQRSTUVWXYZ
abcdefghijklmnopqrstuvwxyzæœfiflffffiffl
&ÆŒ£1234567890,;:.-'!?(

36pt and 24pt

Stevens Shanks Antique 6. About 1860.
From the Figgins foundry. An unmodified
original. Its design changes from size to size.

R Q E N

ABCDEFGHIJKLMN
OPQRSTUVWXYZ
&ÆŒ£1234567890,;:.-'Y

18pt

Stevens Shanks Expanded Antique.
About 1880.
Another type originally from the Figgins
foundry.

RQE
baeg

ABCDEFGHIJ
KLMNOPQRS
TUVWXYZ
abcdefghijklm
nopqrstuvw
xyzæœffffifffiflffifffl
&ÆŒ£12345
67890.,;:-!?"''()

30pt

Stephenson Blake Egyptian Expanded.
About 1860.
A Miller & Richard face bought by
Stephenson Blake around 1950.

RQENbaegn

ABCDEFGHIJKLMNOPQRSTUVWXYZ
abcdefghijklmnopqrstuvwxyzæœfiflffffiffl
&ÆŒ£1234567890,;:.-'!?(

30pt

RQENbaegn

ABCDEFGHIJKLMNOPQRSTUVWXYZ
abcdefghijklmnopqrstuvwxyzfiflffffiffl
&$1234567890.,;:-!?"

30pt

TOP
Stevens Shanks Antique 5. About 1860.
From the Figgins foundry.

BOTTOM
ATF Barnum.
Originally issued by Barnhardt Bros &
Spindler in the nineteenth century.

1840

Clarendons, which first appeared as types in the 1840s, are less challenging in form than egyptians. Serifs are bracketted, proportions more traditional although sometimes condensed, and exaggeration is toned down. To a large extent they are merely an emboldened traditional English vernacular letter: the change from one into the other is barely distinguishable.

These stronger forms were very successful, and could be used as a bold for a condensed modern as, notably, in Baedeker's guide books. Their sturdy construction – bracketted serifs and strong 'thin' strokes – made them (and still make them), in their lighter forms, ideal for rough printing such as on newsprint.

The lack of delicate strokes or fragile serifs has been widely exploited for letters cast in brass or iron, either as an assembled plate, or as individual letters to be applied to the surface. A particularly fine cast clarendon was once famously seen on GWR steam locomotive nameplates. A similar form, given a shadow, was painted on tenders. Other railway companies also used it, again in shadow form; but the GWR was the most consistent in its application, with a tightly controlled style. It was in every way an exemplar. The shiny letters against the green locomotive can be a source of nostalgia, demonstrating the power of good letterforms.

Just as the egyptian is a particularly fine architectural letter, so the clarendon is an engineer's letter. But both are also notable for their effectiveness in print. It is a form that tolerates great freedom of design.

CHARACTERISTICS
Originally bold in weight. Strong bracketted serifs with rounded or square-cut tips. Often very rich forms in their bolder versions, with distinct contrast between thicks and thins; though can be almost monoline. Like the egyptian, can be condensed or expanded successfully.

Stevens Shanks Antique 3

Great Western Railway lettering, Science Museum, London, and National Railway Museum, York.

Britain had a fine tradition of signwritten lettering which has not yet quite died out. Some of the best nineteenth- and twentieth-century examples of this and of cast metal lettering are found in railway museums. The shadowed 'three-dimensional' clarendon painted on GWR tenders is a splendidly worked-out form further enhanced by the painted returns and cast shadows. Nameplates of equal quality consisted of individual brass letters rivetted onto a curved black plate, and fitted to the wheel splashers. These forms are richer and better designed than those of any type equivalent; but the numbers, while having a lot of character, seem slightly less assured. In type, the figures are usually especially good.

North Star, one of four locomotives delivered to the GWR in 1837, had its name in a very similar clarendon. By 1900 this lettering had become refined and was used consistently.

RQENbaegn
baegn

ABCDEFGHIJKLMNOPQRSTUVWXYZ
abcdefghijklmnopqrstuvwxyzfifffflffiffl
&$1234567890.,-:;!?''
ABCDEFGHIJKLMNOPQRSTUVWXYZ
abcdefghijklmnopqrstuvwxyzfifffflffiffl
&$1234567890.,-;:!?''

30pt

ATF Century Schoolbook. 1924, M F Benton.
Derived from the original design of about
1890 by L B Benton for the *Century* magazine.

RQENbaeg
RQENbaeg

Medium and light

ABCDEFGHIJKLMNOPQRSTUVW
XYZabcdefghijklmnopqrstuvwxyz
æœffffifflffiffi&ÆŒ£1234567890.,;:!?-'()
ABCDEFGHIJKLMNOPQRSTUVW
XYZabcdefghijklmnopqrstuvwxyz
ffffiflffiffi&£1234567890.,;:-!?''
ABCDEFGHIJKLMNOPQRSTUVWXYZ
abcdefghijklmnopqrstuvwxyzæœffffiflffiffi
&ÆŒ£1234567890.,;:!?-''()

30pt medium, light, light condensed

Stephenson Blake Consort. 1956-7.
The light and normal versions were revived
from Charles Reed's extended clarendon, cut
by his partner Fox, and registered in 1845.
There are rather elegant condensed and light
condensed versions, and a bold of later date.
The form gets progressively coarser as the
weight increases.

Betws-y-Coed, Gwynedd; Waterloo Bridge, 1815.
Telford's bridge uses 'architectural' lettering in an imaginative and dramatic way. As in the later iron bridge of 1852 at Abermule, Powys, where a fine strong grotesque occupies a similar position and is equally effective, the metal letters are truly part of the bridge structure, not just applied. The first clarendon type appeared in the 1840s, but here is one in 1815, created by an engineer, and there is nothing tentative about the forms. Not as subtly designed as those on GWR locomotives, they are doing a structural job and need to be strong; but as letterforms they seem a little hard. Later types, such as the revival of Consort from 1845, are more subtle and richer. Serifs are longer and letters generally a little wider, giving them more elegance and style.

Dumfries, cast iron plate, 1827.
Somewhat lighter than the GWR clarendon, and with unusually light serifs, these letters are considerably more sensitively designed than those on Waterloo Bridge. They are, like the GWR example, regular and well-fitting; figures, more confident than those for the locomotives, are almost voluptuously rich. Some of the effectiveness of these and GWR cast clarendons is due to the greater difference between thicks and thins than is found in most type clarendons. This, the reverse of what one would have expected of, especially, cast letters, is a characteristic common to most vernacular (non-type) clarendons; they almost seem to belong to a different lettering group. The lettering on Waterloo Bridge is of more even weight than my other examples, more, in this respect, like the type.

It is clear that, in the case of clarendons, the type came after the vernacular form.

RQEN baegn

ABCDEFGHIJKLMNOPQRSTUVWXYZ
abcdefghijklmnopqrstuvwxyzæœfiflfffffiffl
&ÆŒ£1234567890,;:.-'!?(℄

30pt

RQEN baegn

ABCDEFGHIJKLMNOPQRSTUVWXYZ
abcdefghijklmnopqrstuvwxyzæœfffifffiffl
&ÆŒ£1234567890.,:;-!?"()

30pt

TOP
Stevens Shanks Antique 3. About 1860.
The original design from V & J Figgins.

BOTTOM
Stephenson Blake Bold Latin condensed.
About 1884-90.
A Victorian original revived soon after 1928 as
the result of an article in *The Fleuron*. Not cast
from the original matrices but newly engraved
with slight adjustments.

1816

Like the egyptian, the sanserif has history. The same interest in rugged antiquity and the Noble Savage, the same concerns with the character of Greek and Roman buildings and suitable lettering for them, particularly the former, are again behind the new style. Around 1790 John Soane was using a simple monoline and almost geometric sanserif on his drawings; but the first sanserif type, in caps only, made its shy appearance in a type specimen from Caslon, about 1816. It was called, confusingly, an egyptian. It had no progeny until a brutal and ungainly set of caps appeared in 1832 from Figgins.

Sanserifs are largely monoline, which distinguishes them from the more colourful and aggressive grotesques, which began to push them aside. Also, unlike them, their proportions, and sometimes even their basic form, are largely classical, in Gill Sans particularly so. This is really a classic type without serifs; and although of generally even weight, strokes are not entirely equal, and round letters are not always mechanically circular. Even the 'Germanic' Futura, like others of its kind, is not as geometric as it first appears. They all take some liberties with classical form and proportion, and they are not entirely monoline.

The use in architecture of sanserif seems to date from about 1840, although I have seen a small plaque with sanserif carved in relief at Adare, Co Limerick, dated 1831. The relationship of the architectural use of egyptians, sanserifs and grotesques to their appearances in type (and signwriting) is still not clear.

Italian fascist buildings have some good sanserifs, usually in relief, and usually geometric, even 'modernistic'. The pavement of the Vialle del Foro Italico, Rome, has extensive mosaic inscriptions, geometric in form and unclassical in proportion. And Italian State Railways seem to be introducing (in 2006) a slightly redrawn Futura extrabold upper and lowercase for station names and other signs (supplemented by the normal weight) which is surprisingly successful.

CHARACTERISTICS
Serif-less letters of generally classic proportions. Often geometric or semi-geometric in construction, and virtually monoline.

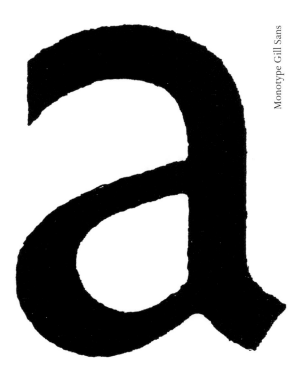

Monotype Gill Sans

W CASLON JUNR   LETTERFOUNDER

Two line English Egyptian

Shire Hall, Brecon, Powys, 1842.
Up to the late eighteenth century, throughout the slow development from venetians to moderns, there was, generally speaking, only one basic letterform in use at any one time, either in type or in other situations. Soon after 1800 this uniformity ended; the several new forms devised to suit new concerns were employed simultaneously in both print and elsewhere. With such diversification, the chronology of type and other letterforms becomes less straightforward. They were all moving along together, if sometimes at different speeds, and starting at different times. In the end, grotesques emerged as the winner.

The first appearance of Caslon's 1816 sanserif was an isolated event, without progeny for some years. Its appearance on buildings was similarly delayed. It may not have been until 1842 that it was used correctly and convincingly, here at Brecon. Only the R looks a little weak; Caslon's is better. His type, too, is better proportioned overall, with the letters more even in width, a feature to be found to a greater or lesser degree throughout these new Victorian styles.

78

RQENbaegn

ABCDEFGHIJKLMNOP
QRSTUVWXYZ
abcdefghijklmnopqrstuvwxyz
&£1234567890.,;:-!?'""''/()

30pt

ABCDEFGHIJKLMNOP
QRSTUVWXYZ
abcdefghijklmnopqrstuvwxyz
&£1234567890.,:;!?''()/--*

30pt New Johnston medium

London Transport Railway Type. 1916, Edward Johnston.
Commissioned by Frank Pick for the exclusive use of London Underground and associated companies. The first of the twentieth-century sanserifs. The proportions are based on classical letterforms, reflecting Johnston's reverence for Trajan roman. In 1979 a major redesign exercise was begun by John Banks and Colin Miles, refining the existing form (every letter was in fact redrawn) and providing new weights and widths: over 500 new forms in all; a distinguished range of types newly worked-out but which keep the spirit of the original. Final artwork for this New Johnston was done by Eiichi Kono.

RQENbaegn
RQENbaegn

ABCDEFGHIJKLMNOPQRSTUVWXYZ
abcdefghijklmnopqrstuvwxyzæœfifffflffiffl
&ÆŒ£1234567890.,;:-!?''()

ABCDEFGHIJKLMNOPQRSTUVWXYZ
abcdefghijklmnopqrstuvwxyzæœfifffflffiffl
&ÆŒ£1234567890.,;:-!?''()

ABCDEFGHIJKLMNOPQRSTUVWXYZ
abcdefghijklmnopqrstuvwxyzæœfifffflffiffl
&ÆŒ£1234567890.,;:-!?''()

30pt bold, medium, light

Monotype Gill Sans. 1928, Eric Gill.
Owing much to Johnston's type, the forms,
again based on classical proportions, are far
subtler and pleasanter. The caps are based on
lettering Gill used for a Bristol bookshop.
Over the years a vast range of weights and
versions was developed. Excellent figures.
After dropping out of fashion a little, its
virtues are becoming appreciated again.
Originally seeming a rather cold type
compared to the colourful Victorian
grotesques, it has an authority and subtlety
which makes most of the 'anonymous' post-
Univers types look anaemic. The Monotype
drawing office made significant contributions
to the design.

For decades Gill meant nothing to
American typographers, and little to the
continental European, who was more
fascinated by the geometry and 'modernism'
of types such as Futura and Erbar.

Mallard, National Railway Museum, York,
1935-7.
Here type and non-type meet. Gill Sans was
issued in 1928. The LNER first used it for
their nameplates in 1934. It was not as well
spaced as GWR's clarendon, although shorter
names were better than the longer ones,
which were often congested-looking yet with
over-wide wordspacing. But when slightly
letterspaced the plates demonstrate what a fine
design Gill is, both as inscription and as type.
It outlives all sanserif rivals, is as valid today
as it ever was. In fact, for text, digitisation has
improved it, especially if the letterspacing is
fractionally tightened in larger text sizes.

RQENbaegn

RQENbaegn

ABCDEFGHIJKLMNOPQRSTUVWXYZ
abcdefghijklmnopqrstuvwxyzæœfffifl
&ÆŒ£1234567890.,;:-!?"'()

ABCDEFGHIJKLMNOPQRSTUVWXYZ
abcdefghijklmnopqrstuvwxyzæœfffifl
&ÆŒ£1234567890.,;:-!?"'()

30pt bold and medium

Bauer Futura. 1927-39, Paul Renner.
The archetypal German 'geometric' sanserif.
Like Gill Sans, produced in a wide variety of
weights and versions. Although less geometric
than it first appears, it has little of the classical
armature found in Gill Sans.

RIGHT
Some letters from Paul Renner's first thoughts
for Futura. These must be some of the ugliest
ideas for a typeface ever. I'm glad he had
second thoughts.

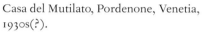

Casa del Mutilato, Pordenone, Venetia, 1930s(?).

Despite the bombastic nature of much of Italian fascist architecture, there is often a purity of form that displays an awareness of the modernism being practiced more imaginatively elsewhere. Slightly vapid, at its best it has a monumental presence which can be effective. The severity of this building is relieved solely by the lettering in bold relief. The form of this is appropriately a geometric sanserif, although it lacks the finesse of Futura. Unyielding, regimented, in its layout and details such as dots between words it attempts to recall Roman inscriptions. The sanserif form has been hijacked for political purposes, a fate the more sensitive Gill Sans could never suffer.

Vialle del Foro Italico, Rome, completed 1936.
This sports complex was designed by Enrico
del Debbio in 1928-31. Here again the sanserif
has become a political tool. In this black-and-
white mosaic pavement, its geometric form

has been manipulated to echo the organised
shouting of a fascist crowd. It is almost
Futurist in its exploitation of letterforms to
onomatopoeic effect. Typeforms, typography
and politics here meet.

1830

Whereas sanserif types are generally more observant of the classic, traditional structure, grotesques have moved into a world of their own. Widths of letters have to some extent been made consistent with one another; shapes are often distorted, especially in the heavier weights (which can be extreme); early versions, those used for Victorian jobbing work, quite abandon accepted ideas of good letter design in their attempts to achieve impact. Although shapes are less extra-ordinary than those of egyptians, which had somehow to incorporate heavy slab serifs, they were looked on askance, even with hatred, by traditionalists (and probably still are). Many of these early grotesques, which were usually in one bold weight, have an individuality, a character, missing from the later regularised forms.

Not until recently considered suitable for bookwork, it was nevertheless *the* typeform of the second half of the twentieth century, particularly promoted by Swiss designers. It is still evolving; but the new fashion seems to be for more effete, thin forms which lack the rich colour of true grotesques, either Victorian or Helvetica. It is not named grotesque for nothing.

Like the egyptians, grotesques have been widely used on buildings, both 'architecture' and vernacular forms such as pubs, chapels, schools or banks, carved or signwritten. It can be cast in metal, and was used in various forms by railway companies other than the GWR for naming their steam locomotives. And of course it is now used almost universally for signage, from motorways and airports, to stations or hospitals. This is not just fashion. It is used because of its clarity, especially now that people have become accustomed to it. Readability of any type has much to do with familiarity.

CHARACTERISTICS
Like the sanserif, could be called an egyptian without serifs. Letter widths more regular and consistent than in classic text types. Extreme weights force more contrast in stroke weights, giving rich and somewhat irregular forms. Weight ranges from ultra-thin to extremely bold; also comes in condensed and expanded versions.

Stephenson Blake Grotesque 8

Unlike romans, grotesques could be designed in innumerable ways, usable in the most varied situations. Between its first appearance as type, about 1830, and 1951, when Helvetica came out, the form was developed to meet modern needs, and is still being developed. These later developments could, as Phil Baines has suggested, be called neo-grotesques. The original divergence from early sanserifs is now less visible: the categories have become blurred. The sanserif/grotesque is the most characteristic form in use today. The aim has always been an ever-closer relationship between the letters, between the wide range of weights which became almost obligatory if the type was to succeed commercially, the condensed versions, the expanded versions.

Twentieth-century versions were deliberately designed to avoid the (appealing) exuberance of earlier grotesques. Opposite can be seen the progression from forceful Victorian grotesques (Thorowgood's seven line grotesque of 1834, the first lowercase grotesque), Royal Gothic of unknown date, possibly the 1870s, to the original Akzidenz Grotesk of 1898 and its refined version of 1962. The latter demonstrates ideas of how this form needed to be rethought for modern work: consistent, carefully related, with cramped forms opened out (e, g), shorter ascenders and descenders. Both versions are 30pt, yet the later one has wider caps and lowercase, but the numerals are narrower.

Checking my paste-up for this book it struck me how rarely used today are the (mostly) Victorian display types that I show: the fatfaces, the egyptians, the clarendons, the pre-Univers grotesques. From the late 1940s until the 1970s the more adventurous publishers in Britain were unafraid to exploit these designs in an unVictorian way: not in pastiche form, but to add typographic colour to twentieth-century structures. Especially notable was the journal *Architectural Review* and the books of its publisher Architectural Press. An inventive yet restrained use of these gamey forms for display was combined with a well-selected variety of colourful non-classical types such as Modern Extended, Ionic or even Clarendon for text, often printed on tinted papers. The result was lively and enticing, although it sometimes had the unfortunate effect of encouraging architects to use typeforms on their buildings – never a happy transformation of use, for type should not be *directly* hijacked this way. The journal especially had a freshness and excitement, a character and individuality, achieving unity in diversity, very different from the bland rather formulaic designs favoured today. It was a different world, *then*, I suppose.

MENINGHURNE
mountainous

Seven line grotesque

ABCDEFGHIJKLMNOPQRSTUVWXYZ
abcdefghijklmnopqrstuvwxyz
&£1234567890.,:;.?!"'()

30pt Stevens Shanks Royal Gothic

ABCDEFGHIJKLMNOPQRSTUVWXYZ
abcdefghijklmnopqrstuvwxyz
&ÆŒ£1234567890.,;:-!?"'()

ABCDEFGHIJKLMNOPQRSTUVWXYZ
abcdefghijklmnopqrstuvwxyzæœfffiflft
&ÆŒ£1234567890.,;:-!?"'()

30pt Berthold Akzidenz Grotesk (Standard) normal and normal series 57

These two examples, of probably roughly the same date, illustrate the extremes of building types for which grotesques were being used.

Sun Terrace, Modbury, Devon.
In absurd contrast to the example opposite is this tiny but unexpectedly effective example. If it were not in strong relief, it would have far less presence. It is a more subtle and richer form than the Hertford example, despite its

diminutive scale, with no trace of geometry in its construction; much more like a typeform. In fact, it could almost be Victorian wood type attached to the building and painted, except, of course, the letters would be back to front.

Corn Exchange, Hertford, 1857.
The architectural style is here Italianate rather than Greek, but the well-designed 'barbaric' letters in strong relief, simple forms of classic and on the whole regular proportions, seem appropriate. Although round characters such as O and C are pure circles, this feels more of a grotesque, rather than a sanserif; but it lacks the subtle changes of thick and thin strokes that grotesque types display. Yet that lack not only makes it more barbaric, but, perhaps, more architectural.

Hardwicke, National Railway Museum, York. LNWR 1873.
Nineteenth-century grotesques, whether in vernacular use or in the form of type, often had a lot of character, with eccentricities which became ironed-out in the twentieth century. The shape of the C here, the short middle stroke of the E, even the low crossbar of the A, are all typical of the period and, as with the type of the time, present a vigorous and self-confident front to the world. The sturdy form with clear contrasts between thicks and thins echoes the characteristics of Stevens Shanks's Royal Gothic, seen on page 87.

RQENbaegn

ABCDEFGHIJKLMNOPQRSTUVWXYZ
abcdefghijklmnopqrstuvwxyz
&£1234567890.,;:-!?'"

30pt

RQENbaegn

ABCDEFGHIJKLMNOPQRSTUVWXYZ
abcdefghijklmnopqrstuvwxyz
&$1234567890.,-:;!?'

30pt

TOP
Stephenson Blake Grotesque 9. 1906, probably
Eleisha Pechey.
One weight only. Characteristic of English
grotesques of this period.

BOTTOM
ATF Franklin Gothic. 1903, M F Benton.
Based on English models. In one weight
originally, although with different widths;
there is now a wide range of weights and
widths in ITC's version of 1979.

RQENbae gn

ABCDEFGHIJKLMNOPQRS
TUVWXYZ
abcdefghijklmnopqrstuvwxyz
&£1234567890.,:;-!?"'()

30pt

Stephenson Blake Grotesque 8. 1898-9,
Eleisha Pechey.
One weight only. Like Grotesque 9,
characteristic of its period, and also of this
typefounder, with tuck-ins to the c, e, r, etc.

RQENbae gn

ABCDEFGHIJKLMNOPQRS
TUVWXYZ
abcdefghijklmnopqrstuvwxyz
æœ fi fl ff ffi ffl & Æ Œ £ 1 2 3 4 5
6 7 8 9 0 . , : ; - ! ? " ' ( )

30pt

Monotype Grotesque Bold Extended. 1921.
Derived from an earlier Miller & Richard
face. Characters like the F, G and R reveal
its origins, but it is generally quite modern
in feeling.

RQEN bae gn

ABCDEFGHIJKLMNOPQRSTUVWXYZ
abcdefghijklmnopqrstuvwxyz
&1234567890 .,:;'-!?()

28D extrabold

Nebiolo Etrusco extrabold. 1960s(?). Aldo
Novarese (?).
A twentieth-century grotesque that exhibits
the spirit of nineteenth-century forms,
although somewhat regularised and more even
in colour. It is worth comparing it with Royal
Gothic (page 87).

OPPOSITE
Relief grotesque, Liverpool.
Harbour Hotel, Haverigg, Cumbria.
The grotesque is the most adaptable of all
letterforms: it can be made thinner, thicker,
wider, narrower, be rounded or angular, while
always retaining its main characteristics. This
has been exploited in the twentieth century to
create large families from the same parent.
The two examples here are very different in
form yet both are archetypal grotesques. The
grubby, gritty letters standing out strongly on

this decayed Liverpool building are bold and
slightly expanded, not unlike Grotesque No 8.
The more condensed letters on Harbour Hotel
are nearer to Grotesque No 9. In these
vernacular forms, the third dimension gives
them additional richness. The wide wordspacing of the hotel lettering makes it look
a little more sophisticated than it really is.
Effective from a hundred yards or more away,
it is, despite or because of its eccentricities, far
more well-mannered than any modern plastic
sign using a crudely adapted typeform.

RQENbaegn
RQENbaegn

**ABCDEFGHIJKLMNOPQRSTUV
WXYZabcdefghijklmnopqrstuv
wxyzæœffffifflffiffl & ÆŒ
£1234567890.,;:-!?"'()**

ABCDEFGHIJKLMNOPQRSTUVWXYZ
abcdefghijklmnopqrstuwvxyz
æœffffiflffiffl&ÆŒ£1234567890.,;:-!?"'()

30D on 36pt

Monotype Grotesque 215 medium and 216
bold. 1926 and 1927.
Of obscure origin, but possibly based on
Wagner & Schmidt's Venus of 1907-27. It has
some late nineteenth-century characteristics.
A much-used precursor of Univers, especially
in Switzerland.

RQENbaegn
RQENbaegn

ABCDEFGHIJKLMNOPQRSTUVWXYZ
abcdefghijklmnopqrstuvwxyzæœ
&ÆŒ£1234567890.,;:-!?''()
ABCDEFGHIJKLMNOPQRSTUVWXYZ
abcdefghijklmnopqrstuvwxyzæœ
&ÆŒ£1234567890.,;:-!?''()

28D on 30pt bold and medium

Monotype Univers. Commenced 1952, Adrian Frutiger.
Originated by Deberny & Peignot, it was designed for both metal and filmsetting as a completely related range of weights and versions. Monotype made minor modifications for hot metal, but more drastic changes for filmsetting, where one set of matrices was used for all sizes from 6 to 22pt. The face was deliberately designed to avoid nineteenth-century associations or a strong personality, so that it could be used unobtrusively or 'anonymously'. As a consequence, display sizes are a little weak. Yet, being conceived from the start as a complete family, it retains its character throughout; unlike many grotesques which had different weights and versions added over the years as commercial expediency required.

RQENbaegn
RQENbaegn

ABCDEFGHIJKLMNOPQRSTUVWXYZ
abcdefghijklmnopqrstuvwxyzæœ
&ÆŒ£1234567890.,;:-!?"()
ABCDEFGHIJKLMNOPQRSTUVWXYZ
abcdefghijklmnopqrstuvwxyz
&ÆŒ£1234567890.,;:-!?"()

30pt medium and normal

Berthold Akzidenz Grotesk. Normal 1898,
light 1902, medium 1909.
Also known as Standard, revised and
regularised versions were brought out in
1962 (series 57 normal, see page 87; series 58
medium). The original version (also shown
here in its normal weight) had characteristic
irregularities much prized by some designers.

RQENbaegn
RQENbaegn

ABCDEFGHIJKLMNOPQRSTUVWXYZ
abcdefghijklmnopqrstuvwxyzæœ
&ÆŒ1234567890.,;:-!?',,"()
ABCDEFGHIJKLMNOPQRSTUVWXYZ
abcdefghijklmnopqrstuvwxyzæœ
&ÆŒ£1234567890.,;:-!?',,"()

28D medium and light

Haas Helvetica. 1951, M Miedinger.
Originally known as New Haas Grotesque,
there is now a revised version (of 1983) called
Neue Helvetica. As with most of the later
twentieth-century grotesques, there is a huge
range of weights and versions. Its relationship
to Akzidenz Grotesk is obvious. The medium
and light versions are still the most successful
of the range.

1928

William Morris began the private press revival, with questionable results as far as the carefully produced books are concerned, but with great effect on the course of printing as a whole. For it drew attention to the generally abysmal printing of the time, with poor types badly printed. At Monotype, Stanley Morison initiated an ambitious and far-reaching programme of new types largely derived from old classics. Simultaneously, entirely new forms were designed as part of that programme. Other type founders followed suit.

It is of course impossible to invent a new typeface devoid of influences. None of these types was based on any particular historical example; but most tend to be more old face in character than modern. Personal preferences of the designer, and national characteristics such as the calligraphic tradition in Germany, are reflected in the designs. Few are widely used today, but Times was and still is immensely successful, and Palatino, today one of the most frequently used text types, is seen here in a slightly lighter variant, Aldus, which appeared a few years later.

CHARACTERISTICS
Varied, but most are economical of space. Modelling from thick to thin strokes gradual. Serifs small, sharply cut, often to a point. Capitals unobtrusive, sometimes considerably lower than ascender height.

Monotype Joanna

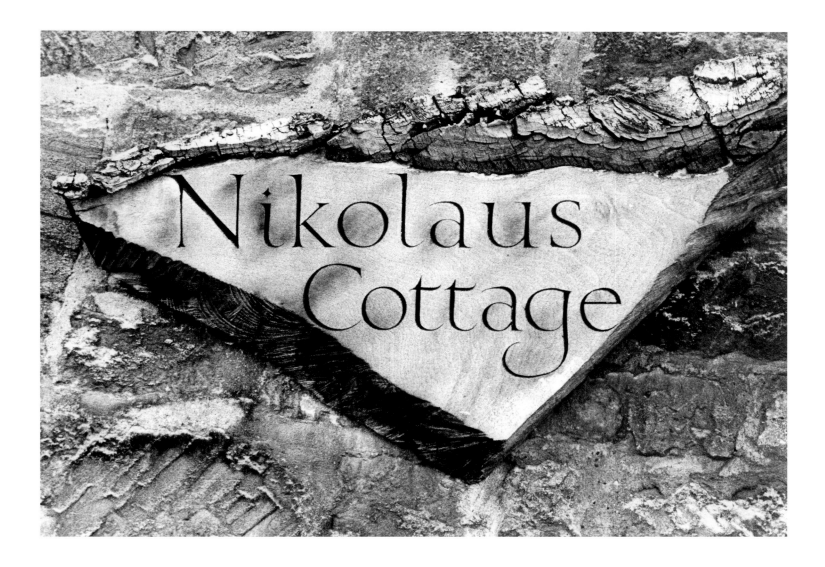

Nikolaus Cottage, Winchcombe, Gloucestershire, 1980s(?).
Many types in the 'twentieth-century' category – original designs not directly derived from classic originals – are traditional in form. So is much of the painted or carved lettering of artist-craftsmen working in the Arts & Crafts tradition. Yet some of the most original of these types were designed by such an artist-craftsman (and sculptor), Eric Gill, disregarding the often tired forms of that tradition.

The letters here, by some anonymous craftsman, show a very personal style. Far removed from any nineteenth-century work, the elegance and originality are also well in advance of respected but very traditional type designers such as Van Krimpen, all of whose types seem, to me, to suffer from defects (see, for instance, Spectrum on page 108). Walter Tracey believed they have never been widely used for this reason. Features that may at first have seemed only slight imperfections can, in time, became major irritations, inhibiting use.

One wonders why a type with obvious defects is ever issued. But the whirligig of time often brings its revenges; for Giovanni Mardersteig's Dante, brought out around the same time as Spectrum, and created within the strict limits of the classical Aldine tradition, is increasingly seen to be a worthwhile addition to the range, its quiet virtues, once seemingly overlooked, now rising in esteem.

Palazzo della Civiltà Italiana, EUR, Rome, 1938-43.
With 56 round-headed openings on each of its four sides, this is a mesmerising building, a de Chirico in three dimensions. There is nothing else on the facades, only the lettering. Although organised in a way reminiscent of that on Roman triumphal arches, its form is more nearly that of the Renaissance, slightly expanded, less elegant, a pastiche without the original conviction; really, just like many twentieth-century types. The extraordinary originality of this building, which becomes almost iconic as the years go by, deserved something better, more surprising. Similarly, many 'original' twentieth-century types are disappointing. It was the revivals by Monotype and others, which were actually based on earlier originals, but convincingly adapted for hot metal and letterpress, which really worked, and transformed printing. This somewhat contradicts the situation today, when the best digital types tend to be original forms designed specifically for the technology.

RQENbaegn
baegn

ABCDEFGHIJKLMNOPQRSTUVWXYZ
abcdefghijklmnopqrstuvwxyzæœfifl
&ÆŒ£1234567890.,;:-!?()
ABCDEFGHIJKLMNOPQRSTUVWXYZ
abcdefghijklmnopqrstuvwxyzæœfifl
&ÆŒ£1234567890.,;:-!?()

30pt PostScript Aldus

Stempel Aldus. 1954. Hermann Zapf.
Originally in 12pt only, the alphabet is
shown here in the 30pt PostScript form.
It is effectively a lighter version of Palatino
by the same designer (1950).

RQENbaegn

baegn

ABCDEFGHIJKLMNOPQRSTUVWXYZ
abcdefghijklmnopqrstuvwxyzæœfiflffffiffl
&ÆŒ£1234567890.,:;-!?''()
ABCDEFGHIJKLMNOPQRSTUVWXYZ
abcdefghijklmnopqrstuvwxyzæœfiflffffiffl
&ÆŒ£1234567890.,:;-!?''()

30pt

Monotype Perpetua. 1928, Eric Gill.
A translation into metal of Gill's sharply-
carved lettering. It retains too much of its
origins for a good text type. It was first cut
by Charles Malin of Paris, not photographed
and pantographed in the usual way. Matrices
were struck, type cast, pulls made; the final
drawings were done from these. While the
capitals are beautiful in large sizes, it is a
rather chilly type.

RQENbaegn
baegn

ABCDEFGHIJKLMNOPQRSTUVWXYZ
abcdefghijklmnopqrstuvwxyzæœfiflffffiffl
&ÆŒ£1234567890.,:;-!?"()
ABCDEFGHIJKLMNOPQRSTUVWXYZ
abcdefghijklmnopqrstuvwxyzæœfiflffffiffl
&ÆŒ£1234567890.,:;-!?"()

30pt

Monotype Joanna. 1930, Eric Gill.
Originally intended for Gill's private press,
Hague & Gill, it was cut by H W Caslon and
Co Ltd. The press was later bought up by
J M Dent, who commissioned a machine
composition version from Monotype in 1937.
It was made generally available in 1958. The
italic is unusually narrow, with only a slight
slope.

RQEN baegn
baegn

ABCDEFGHIJKLMNOPQRSTUVWXYZ
abcdefghijklmnopqrstuvwxyz
&$£1234567890.,-;:!?'()»«·—/
ABCDEFGHIJKLMNOPQRSTUVWXYZ
abcdefghijklmnopqrstuvwxyz
&$£1234567890.,-;:!?'()»«·—/

28D

Weber Schadow-Antiqua. 1938-52,
Georg Trump.
Revealing influences of the German
calligraphic tradition, its underlying
rectilinear character echoing the black letter;
it also has some features found in egyptians,
such as slab serifs. The italic is almost a sloped
roman.

RQEN baegn
baegn

ABCDEFGHIJKLMNOPQRSTUVWXYZ
abcdefghijklmnopqrstuvwxyzæœffffifl
&ÆŒ1234567890.,-:;!?()„"»«/–[]§†*
ABCDEFGHIJKLMNOPQRSTUVWXYZ
abcdefghijklmnopqrstuvwxyzæœffffifl
&ÆŒ1234567890.,-:;!?()„"»«/–[]§†

30pt

Stempel Melior. 1952, Hermann Zapf.
Another original form. Like Schadow-
Antiqua it shows the influence of the German
rectilinear form; there are also hints of a
modern with its vertical stress. The serifs
are strong and horizontal.

RQENbaegn
baegn

ABCDEFGHIJKLMNOPQRSTUVWXYZ
abcdefghijklmnopqrstuvwxyzæœfiflffffifffl
&ÆŒ£1234567890.,:;-!?"'()
ABCDEFGHIJKLMNOPQRSTUVWXYZ
abcdefghijklmnopqrstuvwxyzæœfiflffffifffl
&ÆŒ£1234567890.,:;-!?"'()

28D on 30pt

Monotype Spectrum. 1941-3, Van Krimpen. Designed for Enschedé, originally (though not used) for a range of bibles. This accounts for the smallish, narrow caps. It was not cut until 1952, and brought out by Monotype in 1955. Although in the Aldine tradition, it is a cold type, with a marked contrast between thicks and thins, and rather mean serifs. The a is strangely heavy compared with the other characters; indeed the colour of all the letters is a little uneven. The W is awkward. The italic, based on the calligraphy of Arrighi, seems too narrow for the roman, without having the audacious wilfulness of Joanna's italic. The disturbingly small figures are part of Van Krimpen's original design.

RQENbaegn

baegn

ABCDEFGHIJKLMNOPQRSTUVWXYZ
abcdefghijklmnopqrstuvwxyzæœfiflffffifl
&ÆŒ£1234567890.,:;-!?"'()
ABCDEFGHIJKLMNOPQRSTUVWXYZ
abcdefghijklmnopqrstuvwxyzæœfiflffffifl
&ÆŒ£1234567890.,:;-!?"'()

30pt

Monotype Times. 1932, Stanley Morison, with
Victor Lardent.
Originally designed for *The Times* newspaper.
With its large x-height and quite narrow
letters, it is very economical in space. To some
extent it is a refined and sharpened-up Plantin.
Over-familiarity has made it a little boring,
but it is a practical and well designed type.

Midland Hotel, Manchester, 1898.
Holding their own against the rather over-powering red brick building, these terracotta letters are an architectural manifestation of the kind of decorative type so loved by the Victorians. Like the types, they are splendidly and richly detailed, confident, even brash. The

three-dimensional effect was often simulated in type, although here the face is not only concave, the whole letter is slightly bowed.

Garage, Stafford.
The wild forms of art nouveau govern these
letters. Perverse and distorted, they are not
vulgar despite the giant size and verve.
Designs similar to this and the illustration
opposite can be found in the type of the time;
but not in my selection following.

These four pages show a random selection of decorative types, ranging from about 1700 (Union Pearl) and 1759 (Rosart), through Victorian styles to the latter part of the twentieth century. Bifur was designed by the poster artist A M Cassandre in 1929.

ABCDEFGHIJKLMNOP
QRSTUVWXYZÆŒ.,'°°—

Enschedé Rosart

ABCDEFGHIJKLMNOPQRST
UVWXYZ&1234567890 .,:;'—!9() ᵛᵛᵛ

28D Nebiolo Augusta Filettata

ABCDEFGHIJKLMNOPQRSTUV
WXYZ&£1234567890.,:;-!?'

36pt Stephenson Blake Sans Serif Shaded

ABCDEFGHIJKLMNOPQRST
UVWXYZ&$£1234567890.
,-;:!?'()»«•

28D Weber Forum II

ABCDEFGHIJKLMNOPQRSTUVW
XYZ&£1234567890.,:;-!?'

24pt Stephenson Blake Thorn Shaded

ABCDEFGHIJKLMNOPQRSTUVWXYZ
1234567890.,:-!¨

Deberny & Peignot Lettres Ombrées

ABCDEFGHIJKLMNOPQRSTUVWXYZ
1234567890

Deberny & Peignot Floride

ABCDEFGHIJKLMNOPQRSTU
VWXYZ

30D Olive Calypso

ABCDEFGHIJKLMNOPQRSTUVWXYZ
abcdefghijklmnopqrstuvwxyz
&$1234567890.,;:-!?""()

30pt ATF Comstock

ABCDEFGHIJKLMNOPQRS
TUVWXYZabcdefghijklm
nopqrstuvwxyz&
1234567890$.,-;:!?'{}ˆ

36pt ATF Cooper Hilite

ABCDEFGHIJKLMNOPQRSTU
VWXYZ&$¢1234567890.,;:-!?"

30pt ATF Stencil

ABCDEFGHIJKLMNOPQR
STUVWXYZ&ÆŒ
£1234567890$.,;:'❀⁂„~-!?O

28D Nebiolo Fontanesi

ABCDEFGHIJKLMNOPQRSTUVWXYZ
&ÆŒ1234567890.,;:-!?'«»O

14pt Haas Chevalier

ABCDEFGHIJKLMNOPQRSTUVWXYZ

abcdefghijklmnopqrstuvwxyz . , & ſt b ſh ſ ȷ ð ɡ Qu

22pt Stephenson Blake Union Pearl

ABCDEFGHIJKLMNOPQRSTUVWXYZ
&1234567890,;,

30pt Stevens Shanks Extra Ornamented 2 (Floradora)

ABCDEFGHIJKLMNO
PQRSTUVWXYZ ❧
1234567890.,;::-!?'"❞

36pt ATF Modernistic

114

ABCDEFGHIJKLMNOPQRSTUVWXYZ
abcdefghijklmnopqrstuvwxyzæœfiflff
&ÆŒ£1234567890.,:;!?-"()

24pt Monotype Gill Sans ultrabold

ABCDEFGHIJKLMNOPQRSTUVWXYZ
abcdefghijklmnopqrstuvwxyzæœffffifl
&ÆŒ£1234567890.,;:-!?"()

30pt Bauer Futura black

ABCDEFGHIJKLMNOPQRS
TUVWXYZ
&ÆŒ£1234567890.,;:-!?"()

36pt Deberny & Peignot Bifur

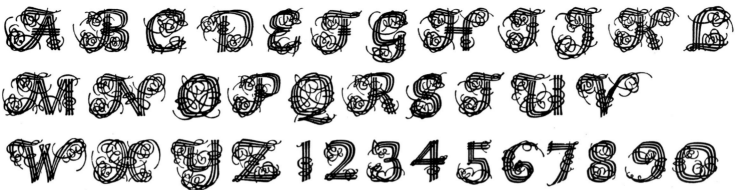

42D on 48pt Amsterdam Raffia Initials

Until the late nineteenth century, punches were cut by hand. The best were masterpieces of precision, equal to the finest engraving in precious metals. In 1884 L B Benton invented a punchcutting machine which, using the pantographic principle, allows the outline of a greatly enlarged copper letter template to be followed, guiding a cutting tool which produces its replica, as a steel punch, in any required size. This punch is then struck in a blank matrix. Into this matrix molten metal was forced through a mould to create a letter.

In a Monotype composing machine for text setting, such matrices were inserted into the matrix case. The latter, placed in the caster, was shuttled around at speed, with its characteristic clanking sound, to site any particular matrix over the mould orifice. Molten metal was injected into the matrix to create the letter. The individual letters were then automatically assembled into lines of text.

One master template was considered insufficient for a full range of sizes in a type family. Enlargement or reduction of the original image affected the balance and proportions of the character, so Monotype modified the template for every third or fourth size, even (for text sizes) every other size. Thus the 30pt alphabets shown in this book are only that: they would produce an inaccurate result if enlarged or reduced in an attempt to create a different size.

The Monotype composition caster produced type from 4.5pt up to 14pt, or up to 24pt with a special attachment. Larger display sizes – the Monotype alphabets shown in this book, for instance – were cast individually on a super caster, and set by hand.

Linotype machines operated on a different system: while the basic sequence of punches, matrices and injection of molten metal into them was followed, the letters were not cast individually then assembled, but were made up into a line before casting.

The design and production of a type family was a lengthy process requiring immense technical precision; yet it presented no serious obstacle to creating any desirable form. The factors governing this remain the same as they always were, and still are: is it printable by the techniques of the day, on the presses, the paper, with the inks; is it legible; is it readable? Do the letters make up well as words? Is it aesthetically pleasing to the taste of the day? Does it reflect the current cultural preferences? Types are the window through which that culture looks. The glass should not distort.

Computer-aided design has reduced the years required to design and produce a family of type down to months. This helps to explain the absurd number of designs gushing out. Most are quickly consigned (deservedly) to oblivion. This is no loss. In the days of letterpress, most designers of text happily made do with less than a dozen types that they felt comfortable with, and often much less. Today, as the dross washes away, at least that number of post-metal types suitable for text remain: quite enough for all normal purposes. The more extrovert requirements of display, where a wider variety is useful, are also well catered for.

If the original of a digital typeface were left in its crude state, it would present a jagged outline on curves and angled strokes; so much technical ingenuity has gone into smoothing out this facetted profile. But while the creation of metal type, although demanding, presented few technical problems, a major problem in the design of digital type is that, for commercial reasons, only one master font is used throughout the full range of sizes (what printer would buy several sizes of font if he could get away with one?); this necessitates a compromise design. If the type has been conceived right from the start for digital form, this drawback can be mitigated, taken into account; but those derived from metal types suffer in this transformation. It is not that the design is changed from the 'sacrosanct' original. Those originals of the 1920s and 1930s were themselves reworked classic faces from earlier centuries, so who are we to complain if they get changed yet again?

It is the unsatisfactory new form which is the problem; and in many cases it is often better to bid a sad farewell to these old friends, which are often too light in text and too coarse or spindly in display. There is a school of thought – not to be dismissed – that today one should only use type designed expressly for digital form and today's technology. This may be an extreme view; but care is needed if ex-metal types are to be used.

Unlike the infinite scale of sizes possible on digital systems, metal type and spacing material was produced in fixed sizes: types were normally 6, 7 (sometimes), 8, 9 (sometimes), 10, 11, 12, 14, 18pt and so on; sizes were occasionally complicated by also coming in Didot (continental) sizes which were 7% larger. Although the use of sizes such as 11.2 on 14.7 was out of the question, this posed no problem at the time. Today such choice adds to the list of lip-chewing decisions (should it be 11.3pt or 11.6pt?). The ingenious designer working with the restrictions of metal usually found a way around them. It could be argued (and I would do so) that the new freedoms in print since the demise of letterpress have contributed to a significant decline in design standards. The constraints and discipline imposed by the mechanics of the old processes concentrated the mind. (Forcing yourself to use restricted means is the sort of restraint that liberates inventing, said Picasso. It obliges you to make a kind of progress you cannot even imagine in advance.) It is no coincidence that the 'Swiss grid' was initially developed in the days of letterpress. While largely a design device to facilitate a desire for precision, order, clarity and intellectual rigour, it also reflected, on paper, the rectangular nature of all the metal components passing through the press.

Throughout the history of printing, changes in the design of type have not only been the consequence of changed printing techniques; sometimes desired design changes have necessitated changes in those techniques. How well does the paper print it? How good are the presses? Does the ink produce the correct result on the paper when run on those presses? The reason John Baskerville is regarded highly now is because he was innovative in so many areas of printing. He devised his own paper and printed by passing it between hot copper cylinders to produce a smoother surface. He formulated his own inks. He developed his own presses to further his aims, and so was able to print his new, sharper letters in a way that showed off their beauty.

The technology of today is continually changing, but the crucial change occurred when letterpress was replaced by offset. Unlike metal types, which were, to a greater or lesser extent, pressed *into* the paper, thickening up the image ('ink squash'), the type image of offset printing sits *on* the paper, with no thickening; which is why so many classic designs can be disappointing when used today. However, since the creation of the early PostScript types, which naturally included those popular classics, digitisation has much improved, engineers having addressed many of the concerns of typographers. A few 'second generation' versions of the classics have been created by typographers, sometimes – pedantically – producing 'authentic' revivals. But typefaces are like people: affected by time, they can develop with age. If the form has sagged a little, some quiet nip and tuck might be beneficial; but all we require is a good usable type, authentic or not.

The following examples are designed to allow comparison of PostScript types with their metal precursors. The 30pt showings of the latter are taken from the Monotype Desk Book of the 1950s and 1960s. Printed on a fairly hard, smooth paper, they show little or none of the ink squash which was allowed for in their design. Thus we see them here in a slightly lighter form than was frequently found at the time they were in use.

Generally, PostScript forms are visually a little larger than their metal equivalents, for x-heights have been increased in relation to cap and ascender heights. Because these showings are for comparing changes in form or weight, I have adjusted the PostScript display sizes to reflect the size of their metal versions by making the x-height the same. In this PostScript form, letters – especially the lowercase – are often wider and more open.

I also compare text settings from books set in hot metal types with the equivalent digital setting. Here, the sizes have not been adjusted. Generally, letters are rather lighter. My hot metal examples have been taken from originals printed by letterpress, and the associated ink squash has thickened the form. PostScript designers curiously omitted to take this effect into account. Of course, different paper, and different print quality, produce different results, far more so than is the case with offset printing. I have chosen what could be described as examples of average printing on typical uncoated letterpress paper.

Becoming expert in the vocation of typesetting
I have equalized my jobs for work excepting that one
ABCDEFGHIJKLMNOPQRSTUVWXYZ

Becoming expert in the vocation of typesetting
I have equalized my jobs for work excepting that one
ABCDEFGHIJKLMNOPQRSTUVWXYZ

What is most striking in the interior of this small but enchanting building is the perfect adaptation of the decoration to the architecture. It is perhaps this marked characteristic of the mosaics of the Mausoleum of Galla Placidia which differentiates them sharply from contemporary Roman mosaics which, divided into square compartments, do not add a mystical sense of the infinite to the classical feeling for space. This is fully achieved, however, in this small building at Ravenna, both by its uninterrupted mosaic surface and by the miraculous harmony of its blues and golds. This effect would not be destroyed if the various charming motives were taken away, such as, for example, the white note formed by the figure of an apostle, or the centre of one of those magical flowers which shine in the vaults.

What is most striking in the interior of this small but enchanting building is the perfect adaptation of the decoration to the architecture. It is perhaps this marked characteristic of the mosaics of the Mausoleum of Galla Placidia which differentiates them sharply from contemporary Roman mosaics which, divided into square compartments, do not add a mystical sense of the infinite to the classical feeling for space. This is fully achieved, however, in this small building at Ravenna, both by its uninterrupted mosaic surface and by the miraculous harmony of its blues and golds. This effect would not be destroyed if the various charming motives were taken away, such as, for example, the white note formed by the figure of an apostle, or the centre of one of those magical flowers which shine in the vaults.

30pt Monotype Bembo, and PostScript version adjusted to the same size.
11 on 12pt hot metal Bembo, and 11 on 12pt PostScript version. Note the long-legged R in the hot metal version creates an awkward space after it.

I have replied to each enquiry about next week
The joint-stock banks might apply a credit squeeze
ABCDEFGHJKLMNOPQRSTUVWXYZ

I have replied to each enquiry about next week
The joint-stock banks might apply a credit squeeze
ABCDEFGHJKLMNOPQRSTUVWXYZ

In Paris, Chagall was not helped by Bakst. But help there came from the poet and animator Guillaume Apollinaire, who went to his studio in 1911 and 1912 and saw there *Me and my Village* (No. 5) and *The Cattle Dealer* (No. 9), and coined the term 'surnatural' (which later became 'surreal') to distinguish them from the expressionist pictures by Rouault and Matisse (then known as 'Fauves') on the one hand, and from the Cubist pictures by Picasso and Braque on the other. At that time Chagall and the Italian Chirico were the first and only 'surreal' painters in the 'School of Paris' (and their work must not be confused with the later Freudian Neo-Surrealist productions of the Breton-Ernst adventure of 1924). *Me and my Village* and *The Cattle Dealer*, though painted in Paris, are wholly built with memory-images of Chagall's native village where one of his family was a cattle dealer and another a rabbi who supervised a slaughter-house and where Chagall, as he has told us in his autobiography, suffered deeply with the slaughtered beasts; and these

In Paris, Chagall was not helped by Bakst. But help there came from the poet and animator Guillaume Apollinaire, who went to his studio in 1911 and 1912 and saw there *Me and my Village* (No. 5) and *The Cattle Dealer* (No. 9), and coined the term 'surnatural' (which later became 'surreal') to distinguish them from the expressionist pictures by Rouault and Matisse (then known as 'Fauves') on the one hand, and from the Cubist pictures by Picasso and Braque on the other. At that time Chagall and the Italian Chirico were the first and only 'surreal' painters in the 'School of Paris' (and their work must not be confused with the later Freudian Neo-Surrealist productions of the Breton-Ernst adventure of 1924). *Me and my Village* and *The Cattle Dealer*, though painted in Paris, are wholly built with memory-images of Chagall's native village where one of his family was a cattle dealer and another a rabbi who supervised a slaughter-house and where Chagall, as he has told us in his autobiography, suffered deeply with the slaughtered beasts; and these

30pt Monotype Garamond, and PostScript version adjusted to the same size.
11pt (solid) hot metal Garamond, and 11pt (solid) PostScript version.

The six documents taking prizes were
Work by Van Dijck equals the greatest
ABCDEGHIJKLMNQRSTUVXYZ

The six documents taking prizes were
Work by Van Dijck equals the greatest
ABCDEGHIJKLMNQRSTUVXYZ

Mrs. Charteris was also suffering from gardener's growing pains. There is something about a garden that brings out a fiercely possessive streak in the best of us. All our triumphs, to be really satisfying, must stem from our own individual efforts; and we look with a cold eye upon innovations for which we are not personally responsible. Even a suggestion, however tactfully introduced, is not always taken in good part. 'Alone I did it,' is the motto of all really keen gardeners; a sentiment which found its modern equivalent in the Army's laconic warning, 'KEEP OUT! THIS MEANS YOU!'

Mrs. Charteris was also suffering from gardener's growing pains. There is something about a garden that brings out a fiercely possessive streak in the best of us. All our triumphs, to be really satisfying, must stem from our own individual efforts; and we look with a cold eye upon innovations for which we are not personally responsible. Even a suggestion, however tactfully introduced, is not always taken in good part. 'Alone I did it,' is the motto of all really keen gardeners; a sentiment which found its modern equivalent in the Army's laconic warning, 'KEEP OUT! THIS MEANS YOU!'

30pt Monotype Plantin, and PostScript version adjusted to the same size.
11 on 13pt hot metal Plantin, and 11 on 13pt PostScript version.

We have now equalized all our jobs for work

A few mixed varying size blocks pique the judges

ABCDEFGHJKLMNOPQRSTUVWXYZ

We have now equalized all our jobs for work

A few mixed varying size blocks pique the judges

ABCDEFGHJKLMNOPQRSTUVWXYZ

The notion of art that was expressed throughout the Great Exhibition of 1851 was of something that is sumptuous: stupid and clumsy forms did not seem to matter, so long as they bristled with ornament, to suggest the opulence of the owner and to hint that he, too, like the aristocracy of the past, could afford to go in for magnificence. Please remember that this attitude of mind was largely subconscious. Most of the people who succumbed to it were diligent and worthy folks, who had given no clear thought to any question of the beautiful, because they were occupied with other things. The contagion of false ideas is very insidious. They creep into the best regulated families, and the baseness of their origin is seldom recognized. *Once fall into the habit of accepting outward show in the place of living art, and it will persist. Nothing will*

30pt Monotype Baskerville, and PostScript version adjusted to the same size.
11 on 12pt hot metal Baskerville, and 11 on 12pt PostScript version.

The notion of art that was expressed throughout the Great Exhibition of 1851 was of something that is sumptuous: stupid and clumsy forms did not seem to matter, so long as they bristled with ornament, to suggest the opulence of the owner and to hint that he, too, like the aristocracy of the past, could afford to go in for magnificence. Please remember that this attitude of mind was largely subconscious. Most of the people who succumbed to it were diligent and worthy folks, who had given no clear thought to any question of the beautiful, because they were occupied with other things. The contagion of false ideas is very insidious. They creep into the best regulated families, and the baseness of their origin is seldom recognized. *Once fall into the habit of accepting outward show in the place of living art, and it will persist.*

Expect equal workings of demy size jobs
The work of Van Dijck equals the greatest
ABCDEFGHIJKLMNOPQRSTUVWXYZ*AB*

Expect equal workings of demy size jobs
The work of Van Dijck equals the greatest
ABCDEFGHIJKLMNOPQRSTUVWXYZ*A*

Noteworthy features. Exterior: (1) The detached bell-tower adjoining the choir is Romanesque in its lower sections; the octagonal part added partly in seventeenth, partly in eighteenth century. (2) The turrets over the transepts are unusual and of doubtful significance. *Interior:* (1) The nave design is hard to classify. The ground arcades suggest a basilical form and the side-aisles have their own vaults. But above them is a second arcade storey and the upper side vaults are of equal height with the central. Apparently a hall church with a balustraded gallery running along sides and round W. end separating ground from upper arcades. (2) Between each pair of lower and upper columns flat pilaster strips are applied to the wall, seemingly to give the impression of continuity between the two arcades. (3) The general feeling is perhaps Gothic rather than Baroque, a feeling enhanced no doubt by the black (Melchthal) marble used to pick out columns, arches, pilasters and balustrade, and

Noteworthy features. Exterior: (1) The detached bell-tower adjoining the choir is Romanesque in its lower sections; the octagonal part added partly in seventeenth, partly in eighteenth century. (2) The turrets over the transepts are unusual and of doubtful significance. *Interior:* (1) The nave design is hard to classify. The ground arcades suggest a basilical form and the side-aisles have their own vaults. But above them is a second arcade storey and the upper side vaults are of equal height with the central. Apparently a hall church with a balustraded gallery running along sides and round W. end separating ground from upper arcades. (2) Between each pair of lower and upper columns flat pilaster strips are applied to the wall, seemingly to give the impression of continuity between the two arcades. (3) The general feeling is perhaps Gothic rather than Baroque, a feeling enhanced no doubt by the black (Melchthal) marble used to pick out columns, arches, pilasters and balustrade, and

30pt Monotype Walbaum, and PostScript
version adjusted to the same size.
10 on 12pt hot metal Walbaum, and 10 on 12pt
PostScript version.

The metal version of 14pt is shown on the
right, together with its PostScript equivalent.
Above 14pt, the metal version changes in
design and weight to become, effectively,
a semibold.

When jobs have their type sizes fixed
When jobs have type sizes fixed quickly
ABCDEFGHJKLMNOPQRSTUWZ

When jobs have their type sizes fixed
When jobs have type sizes fixed quickly
ABCDEFGHJKLMNOPQRSTUWZ

Expect equal workings of all demy size jobs
Work by Van Dijck equals the greatest
ABCDEFGHJKLMNOPQRSTUVWXYZ*A*

Expect equal workings of all demy size jobs
Work by Van Dijck equals the greatest
ABCDEFGHJKLMNOPQRSTUVXYZ*A*

And without hurrying he went on his way. At the corner of the wood, in between two white posts, appeared a drive which Meaulnes entered. He walked up a few yards and stopped startled, disturbed by inexplicable feelings. He walked with the same fatigue, the icy wind cut his lips and took his breath away, and yet a strange contentment urged him on, **a** perfect and almost intoxicating peace, the assurance that his goal had been reached and that he had now nothing but happiness to expect. In the same way he once used to feel faint with excitement on the eve of great summer festivals, when fir trees, whose branches overshadowed his bedroom window, were set up at nightfall along the village streets.

And without hurrying he went on his way. At the corner of the wood, in between two white posts, appeared a drive which Meaulnes entered. He walked up a few yards and stopped startled, disturbed by inexplicable feelings. He walked with the same fatigue, the icy wind cut his lips and took his breath away, and yet a strange contentment urged him on, a perfect and almost intoxicating peace, the assurance that his goal had been reached and that he had now nothing but happiness to expect. In the same way he once used to feel faint with excitement on the eve of great summer festivals, when fir trees, whose branches overshadowed his bedroom window, were set up at nightfall along the village streets.

30pt Monotype Bodoni, and PostScript
version adjusted to the same size.
10 on 12pt hot metal Bodoni, and 10 on 12pt
PostScript version.

Speed and skill in the art of engraving
All the equipment was skilfully improvised
ABCDEGHJKLMNOPQRSTUVWXYZ

Speed and skill in the art of engraving
All the equipment was skilfully improvised
ABCDEGHJKLMNOPQRSTUVWXYZ

30pt Monotype Gill Sans, and PostScript version adjusted to the same size.
9 on 11pt hot metal Gill Sans, and 9 on 11pt PostScript version.

The term 'concentration on the real problems' of sculpture has been used a moment ago. But what are the real problems of sculpture, if they are not a rendering of the human form? If the public is so much less conscious of them than it is of those of painting, this is due to the fact that the nineteenth century was a century of painting. Hence we tend to look at sculpture in two dimensions. Some works, it is true, can be appreciated in the way a painting or a drawing is, that is in the flat, *e.g.*, Eric Gill's *Deposition* which is essentially an exquisite silhouette (see the arm cut off above the head). But the rule is that one can only do justice to sculpture if one sees it in depth as well as in height and breadth. The three-dimensional effect may be primarily one of solid volume in opposition to the space, our space, surrounding it; this is, for instance, the case in McWilliam's harassing *Head* in two monoliths (in which the seemingly arbitrary cutting out of parts and erecting them in front of us tends to let us see these parts overwhelmingly intensified, because over-focused.

The term 'concentration on the real problems' of sculpture has been used a moment ago. But what are the real problems of sculpture, if they are not a rendering of the human form? If the public is so much less conscious of them than it is of those of painting, this is due to the fact that the nineteenth century was a century of painting. Hence we tend to look at sculpture in two dimensions. Some works, it is true, can be appreciated in the way a painting or a drawing is, that is in the flat, e.g., Eric Gill's *Deposition* which is essentially an exquisite silhouette (see the arm cut off above the head). But the rule is that one can only do justice to sculpture if one sees it in depth as well as in height and breadth. The three-dimensional effect may be primarily one of solid volume in opposition to the space, our space, surrounding it; this is, for instance, the case in McWilliam's harassing *Head* in two monoliths (in which the seemingly arbitrary cutting out of parts and erecting them in front of us tends to let us see these parts overwhelmingly intensified, because over-focused.

Epilogue

For five centuries the roman alphabet has changed its surface appearance in type, on architecture and in vernacular use. Its life began, of course, over 1000 years earlier (to put it cautiously) with Roman inscriptions which were using letters recognisably 'ours'. These forms had been derived from Greek scripts.

Letters are an invention comparable to the wheel, and in some ways more important. These symbols can permanently record events which would otherwise be lost or become distorted in memory. And the history and achievements of earlier times, and ours, could disappear entirely without the record that these letters allow.

These symbols not only make sense when looked at, they can be converted into sound, or speech. Grouped together they can build up ideas of immense complexity, or beauty, or subtlety, or outrage. They order us, help us, guide us, inform us, entertain us, enable us to navigate life and the world with precision and, to a large extent, certainty. If there is uncertainty or lack of clarity, it is not the fault of the letters, it is how they are put together.

Yet these symbols can be transformed visually without any loss of their essential character. The changes reflect new societies, new technologies, new preferences, new functions; but within these changes the symbols are constant, always themselves. Compare a Bembo letter with a fatface letter. They seem completely different symbols. Their effect on the viewer is quite different; they suggest quite different undertones of meaning; yet in essence they are the same.

Such undertones can be exploited to suggest intangible meanings or ideas beyond the range of mere words. The Futurists treated type in a cavalier fashion in order to give additional graphic force to the words of their poems. Lessons can still be learnt from the way they used letterforms to elucidate or intensify meaning. Most of the 26 symbols shown here in so many different forms look innocuous, genteel, as harmless as rows of old ladies. Yet (just like some old ladies) within them they contain dynamite, the power to destroy or create.

They talk to us from the pages in our hands, from buildings in the street, from shops, from signs. When we work with them we must choose them carefully and thoughtfully. The typeface is a conduit for the text. The reader's reaction to this can be coloured by the character of the type, just as it can be by the typographic treatment. Moreover, types have a history, they have associations, a hidden power. Marinetti and his fellow Futurists used different sizes, weights and styles of type within the same work, even the same word, to further their aims. (See the example on page 1.) He believed it mattered little if a deformed word seems ambiguous at first. Its abstract expression of an emotion or thought can quickly be understood through its context.

The main purpose of this book is not to produce a new generation of Futurists. The intention is to open the windows of the reader's mind to the potential contained within these symbols that we take so much for granted. It highlights the subtle visual differences that can be exploited to enhance communication; it provides a historical narrative and context; it gives the wider background which adds further resonance to the letters. All of which helps to extend our understanding of this rich pool of material with which we work.

The alphabet has created our memory, and thus our civilisation. It has been a long journey from Subiaco.

Bibliography

TYPE AND CALLIGRAPHY

P Baines & A Haslam	*Type and Typography*. London 2005
C Banks	*New Johnston (in Typos 1)*. London n.d. 1980?
A Bartram	*Five Hundred Years of Book Design*. London 2001
A Bartram	*Futurist Typography & the Liberated Text*. London 2005
G Bickham	*The Universal Penman 1743*. New York 1968
R Bringhurst	*The Elements of Typographic Style*. Vancouver 1992
D Bullough	*The Age of Charlemagne*. London 1965
S Carter	*Twentieth Century Type Designers*. London 1987, 1998
K Cheng	*Designing Type*. London 2006
M Davies	*Aldus Manutius*. London 1995
G Dowding	*An Introduction to the History of Printing Types*. London 1961, 1998
A Fairbank	*A Book of Scripts*. Harmondsworth 1949
A Gaur	*A History of Writing*. London 1984
A Glaister	*Glaister's Glossary of the Book*. London 1979 reprinted as *Glaister's Encyclopedia of the Book*. London 1996
N Gray	*The Painted Inscriptions of David Jones*. London 1981
P M Handover	*Letters Without Serifs (in Motif 6)*. London 1961
C P Hornung	*Handbook of Early Advertising Art, typographical volume*, New York 1956
W Jaspert et al	*The Encyclopedia of Typefaces*. London 1962, 1970, 1983
J Lewis	*Printed Ephemera*. Ipswich 1962
N Macmillan	*An A-Z of Type Designers*. London 2006
H Meyer	*The Development of Writing*. Zurich 1969
S Morison	*Four Centuries of Fine Printing*. London 1924, 1949, 1960
S Morison	*Selected Essays on the History of Letterforms*. Cambridge 1981
D Sacks	*The Alphabet*. London 2003
R Southall	*Printer's Type in the Twentieth Century*. London 2005
H Spencer	*The Visible Word*. London 1968
H Spencer (ed)	*Typographica (magazine)*. London 1949-67
S Steinberg/J Trevitt	*Five Hundred Years of Printing*. London 1996
J Sutton & A Bartram	*An Atlas of Typeforms*. London 1968
J Sutton & A Bartram	*Typefaces for Books*. London 1990
W Tracy	*Letters of Credit*. London 1986
M Twyman	*Printing 1770-1970*. London 1970, 1998
D B Updike	*Printing Types: their history, forms & use*. Cambridge Ma 1922, 1937; London 2001
L W Wallis	*Modern Encyclopedia of Typefaces 1960-90*. London 1990
J I Whalley	*The Pen's Excellencie. Calligraphy of Western Europe & America*. Tunbridge Wells 1980

ARCHITECTURAL/VERNACULAR LETTERING

P Baines & C Dixon	*Signs: Lettering in the environment*. London 2003
A Bartram	*Lettering in Architecture*. London 1975
A Bartram	*Tombstone Lettering in the British Isles; Fascia Lettering in the British Isles; Street Name Lettering in the British Isles*. All London 1978
A Bartram	*The English Lettering Tradition from 1700 to the present day*. London 1986
P Burridge	*Nameplates of the Big Four including British Railways*. Oxford 1975
N Gray	*Sans Serif and other experimental inscribed lettering of the early Renaissance (in Motif 5)*. London 1960
N Gray	*Lettering on Buildings*. London 1960
N Gray	*A History of Lettering*. Oxford 1986
J Kinnear	*Words & Buildings*. London 1980
J Mosley	*English Vernacular (in Motif 11)*. London 1963
J Mosley	*The Nymph & the Grot*. London 1999
F Salmon	*Building on Ruins: the rediscovery of Rome and English architecture*. Aldershot 2000
H Spencer (ed)	*Typographica (magazine)*. London 1949-1967
J Sutton	*Signs in Action*. London 1965
P Williams	*Britain's Railway Museums*. London 1974

There may be later editions of some of the books listed here

Index